RECOGNIZING RELIGION IN
A SECULAR SOCIETY

Recognizing Religion in a Secular Society

Essays in Pluralism, Religion, and Public Policy

Edited by

DOUGLAS FARROW

McGill-Queen's University Press
Montreal & Kingston · London · Ithaca

© McGill-Queen's University Press 2004
ISBN 0-7735-2812-1 (cloth)
ISBN 0-7735-2834-2 (paper)

Legal deposit third quarter 2004
Bibliothèque nationale du Québec

Printed in Canada on acid-free paper that is 100% ancient forest free
(100% post-consumer recycled), processed chlorine free.

This book has been published with the help of a grant from the Canadian
Federation for the Humanities and Social Sciences, through the Aid to
Scholarly Publications Programme, using funds provided by the Social
Sciences and Humanities Research Council of Canada.

McGill-Queen's University Press acknowledges the support of the Canada
Council for the Arts for our publishing program. We also acknowledge
the financial support of the Government of Canada through the Book
Publishing Industry Development Program (BPIDP) for our publishing
activities.

National Library of Canada Cataloguing in Publication

Recognizing religion in a secular society: essays in pluralism, religion and
  public policy/edited by Douglas Farrow.
  Includes papers first presented at the Pluralism, Religion and Public Policy
  Conference, held Oct. 9–11, 2002 at McGill University.
  Includes bibliograhical references and index.
  ISBN 0-7735-2812-1 (bnd)
  ISBN 0-7735-2834-2 (pbk)
  1. Religion and politics – Congresses. 2. Religion and state – Canada –
  Congresses. 3. Religions – Social aspects – Canada – Congresses.
  4. Pluralism (Social sciences) – Canada – Congresses. I. Farrow, Douglas,
  1953–. II. Pluralism, Religion and Public Policy Conference
  (2002: McGill University).
  BL65.P7R37 2004   322′.1′0971   C2004-901773-X

Typeset in New Baskerville 10/13
by Caractéra inc., Quebec City

for
CLAUDE RYAN
1925–2004
with gratitude for his faithful
contribution to public life

Contents

In Place of a Foreword

"There has been a tendency since World War II to relegate religion to the private sphere; to suggest that it should have as little as possible to do with economic, social, and political life. This approach appeared to succeed for a time. But religion, in my opinion, cannot be confined indefinitely to the private sphere...*

It is possible in principle to make distinctions between those things that belong to the temporal order and those that pertain to the spiritual order, but in practice – in actual relations between human beings – that is not the way the problem poses itself. Issues of right and wrong inevitably arise whenever human beings are brought together. Neither the actions of individuals nor those of public authorities can be totally immune from moral implications. On the contrary, debates are bound to arise, and arise all the time, about a wide range

---

* Editor's note: Mr Ryan refers us for guidance to St Augustine, whose monumental work, *The City of God*, was his own major inspiration respecting the complex relation between religion – which is "both personal and social, private and public" – and secular society. He then comments on pursuit of the common good as well as on the importance of freedom of religion, insisting that "things that matter to horizons which reach beyond the present world must remain independent of the reach of public authority."

of issues having moral ramifications, and this as soon as life in society exists.

In light of this, the idea of a completely valueless society must be rejected as untenable, though it is the unwritten premise upon which rests many of the affirmations that we hear nowadays. A valueless society is unthinkable. Human nature being essentially moral, a life without any reference to moral principles would simply not be human. We must also rule out the idea of a society in which only the values geared to each individual, or even to a majority, would be worthwhile. A set of commonly accepted moral values is indispensable for the good operation of every society.

Some difficult questions must be faced, however. If there must necessarily be a reference to moral values in political life, should the reference be to specific objective values, and if so, should someone be entitled to define those values on behalf of the entire society or should societal choices be made solely on the basis of the state of public opinion at a given point in time? These are not easy questions; there are no easy and uniform answers to them. It is possible, however, to project a little light on how they could be dealt with in a democratic society.

According to a widespread view, debates on controversial issues with strong moral implications should take place and be resolved in the absence of specific reference to religion. The justification of this position is that religion is divisive; that the views of religious people on many questions sometimes rest upon shaky intellectual foundations. According to an opposite opinion, religion is the safest guardian of moral values in human society. It cannot in consequence remain silent, or accept that it be ignored in decisions in which moral values are implied.

For those who hold the first opinion, silence or at least restraint on the part of religious believers is more likely to foster social peace. But obliging some people to keep their opinions to themselves is in itself (when one thinks of it) an intolerant, fundamentally undemocratic way of buying harmony among citizens of a free society. However we find it may look on the surface, this so-called "liberal" approach, which is not truly

liberal in my opinion, is a thinly veiled way of curtailing the
freedom of expression of religious believers. While it may
present practical advantages, it is unacceptable in principle.

On the other hand, modern societies being more and more
pluralist from a religious point of view, no one church can
expect that its views on controversial issues will be retained by
all for the sole reason that it holds them to be true. In a
democratic society, public debates will take place around such
issues which will sooner or later be followed by decisions that
will be binding upon all, even though they may not accord
with the views of some groups. They must be accepted. But
there is one reservation here: once a political decision has
been made, it should not mean the end of the debate! The
debate must continue, and it may happen that through intelligent work public opinion will eventually change and bring
leaders to other decisions. That is the virtue of the political
process. The democratic process is an unending one. There is
very seldom a final answer to any question, and it must remain
that way."

CLAUDE RYAN*

---

* A short excerpt from his presentation in the opening session of
the "Pluralism, Religion and Public Policy" conference, McGill
University, 9 October 2002. A full recording is available.

Acknowledgments

The present volume represents one stream of the conversation that began in Montreal at the "Pluralism, Religion and Public Policy" conference, October 2002, which was co-sponsored by McGill University's Faculty of Religious Studies and the Centre for Cultural Renewal in Ottawa. It owes much also to the many other partners, whether sponsors or speakers or delegates, who helped to make that rare event the remarkable success it was. (The support of the Beatty Memorial Lectures Committee, and of the Human Security Division of the Department of Foreign Affairs and International Trade, is worthy of special mention.) What a privilege it was to see philosophers, theologians, historians, jurists, politicians, civil servants, doctors, clerics, psychologists, social scientists – several hundred professionals and students from across North America – engage together in three solid days of sustained debate. What is contained here is offered by some of the participants in that debate not as a record (which it is not) but, rather, as a tribute and a stimulus to conversations yet to come.

DOUGLAS FARROW, McGill University
IAIN T. BENSON, Centre for Cultural Renewal

Introduction

"Recognizing religion in a secular society," unlike the similar sounding title used by Bryan Wilson in the sixties, is a deliberately ambiguous turn of phrase. It might be a plea or even a demand. It might be a warning or perhaps an accusation. It might simply be a task, whether interesting or onerous. In this book it is all of the above, as you will see soon enough – with the exception, we think, of the onerous. Here is a concise and potent set of essays by influential theorists and practitioners who find their subjects anything but onerous.

Their expertise, like their philosophical, political, and religious commitments, is varied. But their interests intersect at the point where concern for the common good, and for the political and legal structures that serve that good, touch on the question of religion. Wilson, who observed that modern secular society "has little direct regard for religion" and "does not appear to depend in any direct way on the maintenance of religious thinking, practices, or institutions," anticipated that we would see "the still persisting influence of past religion [wane] even further."[1] This prophecy, though in some sense self-fulfilling, has proved only half right. Many sociologists are persuaded that religion is as much a force today as ever it was, though there can be no doubt that the religious landscape and the trajectories of religious influence have altered

1 *Religion in Secular Society*, 228, 233.

substantially.[2] Some will even argue that the process of secularization that has tended to mute religious voices has been an artificial rather than a natural one.[3]

There are grounds, then, for making the plea that religion is too little acknowledged in the public realm or, at all events, that it is too little understood, as H.R.H. Prince El Hassan bin Talal (moderator of the World Conference on Religion and Peace) already makes clear in Chapter 1. Pointing out the relation between religion, ethics, human solidarity, and good governance, he attempts to show that Islam in particular – one of today's most controversial religions – deserves better and more sympathetic attention than it sometimes gets.[4] Subsequent essayists concern themselves with one or another feature of the relational nexus just mentioned, and they do so, like Prince Hassan, in the light of their own direct engagement in that nexus.

In Chapter 2 the Right Honourable Beverley McLachlin, Chief Justice of Canada, takes up the problematic relation between freedom of religion and the rule of law in the context of the Charter of Rights and Freedoms. This will doubtless prove one of the book's most controversial chapters, not least because of its premise (adopted from Yale professor Paul Kahn) that the law is like religion in making a comprehensive claim on human experience. Chief Justice McLachlin argues that the paradox of two total claims to authority can be (and in Canada, at least, generally has been) resolved happily as the law carves out an appropriate public space for the free exercise of faith. This approach to a resolution does of course imply that the comprehensiveness in question is not the same in each case and that the law has priority in the public realm whereas religion has priority in the private realm. That is a thesis challenged, together with its premise, by the quite different analysis of her well known respondent from the University

---

2 See, for example, Casanova, *Public Religions in the Modern World*, on which see further the editorial postscript below.

3 Compare Smith, ed., *The Secular Revolution*.

4 Compare also Hashmi, ed., *Islamic Political Ethics*.

of Chicago, Jean Bethke Elshtain, which has been included as an addendum to Chapter 2. Professor Elshtain, who regards religion too as a public matter,[5] champions a non-litigious dialectic of *citizens* rather than a dialectic of law and religion.

The next two essays represent a continuation of this debate, albeit without direct reference to it. In Chapter 3, Professor William Galston (sometime advisor to President Clinton and director of the Institute for Philosophy and Public Policy in Washington) argues powerfully for "a politics of recognition rather than of construction," and for a pluralist polity that pursues not a comprehensive but a partial good. The state, he maintains, being a secondary or even a tertiary rather than a primary form of human sociality, ought to accept for itself a carefully circumscribed role. In Chapter 4, Rabbi David Novak, the prolific political and religious theorist from the University of Toronto, develops the same theme, contending for the priority of primal communities (familial and religious) over contractual or civil society. This involves a fundamental reorientation of social contract theory and has enormous implications for jurisprudence as well as for political life. These two chapters lie at the heart of *Recognizing Religion in a Secular Society* by virtue of their respective attempts to cut to the core question of what society actually is and how it comes to be – for it is only in that context that the question of the role of religion in society, and of its relation to the state and to the law, can be addressed properly. In weighing up the contribution of this volume to public debate about such things, it will have to be decided how far their approaches and conclusions are compatible with each other but, more especially, how far they are compatible with the approach represented by Chief Justice McLachlin.

Jean Elshtain returns in Chapter 5 with an essay of her own, based on her recent Birks Lecture at McGill, in which she makes a case for recovering the deep structure of human rights language, without which the whole essential culture of

---

5 That is, not "merely a matter for private predilection," as Wilson puts it (*Religion in Secular Society*, 229).

rights may prove to be unsustainable. The language of human rights, as many are beginning to notice, has of late become over-inflated, in a bid to absorb or sublate or even supplant traditional realms of theological, political, legal and social discourse. It is a currency in danger of collapse, a collapse made more imminent by the fact that this discourse seems so much hot air in the face of persistent, egregious violations of human freedom and dignity. What Professor Elshtain attempts here is a return to basics, basics which have been ignored because they necessitate dealing with ideas uncomfortable to a certain kind of secularism – the kind that fears religion. In Chapter 6 Iain Benson, a constitutional lawyer, traces the emergence of secularism as a set of essentially anti-religious conceptions by way of reference to the work of the man who coined the term, George Jacob Holyoake. He follows up by illustrating the impact of such secularism on jurisprudential debates about the meaning of the term "secular" (a term that the Supreme Court of Canada has recently interpreted in a religion-inclusive way).

Chapters 7 and 8 may at first glance appear to be a diversion. They are not. They serve rather to heighten the tension already created by the preceding chapters. For if the inner space of biotechnology represents a frontier as exciting and as dangerous – almost certainly *more* dangerous – for humanity as that of outer space, then it also represents a profoundly important intersection between religion, public policy, and the law. Margaret Somerville, founding director of the McGill Centre for Medicine, Ethics and Law, sets the stage by way of a frank assessment of the challenges to the sanctity of life posed – often in the name of human dignity – by emergent practices in genetics and in geriatrics: that is, at the margins of human life, where it is most vulnerable. She concludes with a cautious, Habermasian call for a re-engagement between science and technology, on the one hand, and the spiritual wisdom of the great religious traditions on the other.

H. Tristram Engelhardt, Jr, one of the builders of modern bioethics, tacks in the opposite direction. Searching for moral consensus after "the cultural death of God," he argues, is like chasing a mirage. The best we can hope for is the means (those proper to a limited democracy) to live peaceably in spite of fundamental and irresolvable moral differences. Professor Engelhardt's essay, which serves as a warning against attempts to paper over the cracks between the religions, as well as between the religious and the non-religious, will for some be as controversial as is Beverley McLachlin's. It is not inappropriate that these two essays (with their common yet conflicting commitments to pluralism and to the procedural republic) should stand more or less at opposite ends of the volume, marking out the territory in between as the field of engagement.

As there was a first essay, however, so there is a last. It too contains a warning – more, perhaps, like the one we are so used to hearing today – a warning that says: "Beware, lest religion corrupt and destroy the hard-won liberties of our secular society, subjecting us to the slavery of some new or old theocracy." Bringing to the foreground a motif present in the background of several of the earlier chapters, Chapter 9 almost dares an accusation. But the religious culprit it fingers is not the usual one. With Rousseau's assistance, it charts a course that leads back to the Charter of Rights and Freedoms, though to say more here would be to say too much.

For the moment, it need only be added that none of these essayists – be they Muslim, Jewish, Roman Catholic, Orthodox, Protestant, agnostic, or whatever – adopts towards religion the quietly superior stance of a Bryan Wilson. Which is to say, none of them, as a matter of course, associates religion with mere emotion or with "irrational and arbitrary assumptions about life, society and the laws which govern the physical universe."[6] That does not make them apologists for religion,

---

6 Wilson hastens to add, with deepest irony, that he does not employ the concept of secularization "in any ideological sense," as if "to applaud its occurrence" or "to deplore it" (ibid., x, xi)! How indeed could one either applaud or deplore "the process of man's increasing rationality" or "his recognition of 'real facts'" (231)?

any more than it prevents them from recommending this or
that religion should they so choose. Certainly it does not guarantee that their observations will be more trenchant, or less,
than those of Wilson's persuasion. It does, however, help to
qualify them – their other qualifications will be evident – as
sympathetic analysts of the relation between religion and secular society: a relation far too important to leave entirely to
the sociologists.

EDITOR

RECOGNIZING RELIGION IN
A SECULAR SOCIETY

I

Religion in the Public Realm

H.R.H. PRINCE EL HASSAN BIN TALAL

Modernity, on some accounts, would permanently remove religion from the public square. Even when we try to balance religion with other participants in the public realm, we often do so with the assumption that religion per se shares nothing, as an idea or even as an experience, with the pluralism, liberalism, and secularism that are regarded as the mutually defining criteria of modern democratic societies. Globalism, too, has sometimes been approached through concepts that have tended to relegate religion to the sidelines or to a past era. Thus religion is seen as neither good nor bad but, rather, as irrelevant because our understanding of it in the postindustrial world of material and social advancement does not require it to be part of the overall human equation.

We may pause to ask, however, whether and how the values that underlie our most cherished notions – notions such as human dignity or human rights, for example – can be sustained today in ways that will "guide effectively our legislators, judges, and those charged with overseeing public welfare."[1] And if we wish to answer in the affirmative, and give substance to our answers, then we are driven to the consideration of

---

1 This was one of the thematic questions put to participants in the "Pluralism, Religion, and Public Policy" conference at McGill University (October 2002).

ethical imperatives. In this context it must be assumed from the outset that religion, which seeks to embody those spiritual values that humanity generally holds so dear, already plays a determining role in developing and promoting an ethical perspective and code of conduct.

For this reason, among others, we ought to acknowledge the relevance of religion to our own age and challenge assumptions (usually found within the postindustrial countries) of its irrelevance. Authentic religion actually provides a way of engaging new ideas or philosophies, integrating them with the wisdom of the past. It also provides a means for recognizing the common ground that is created through acknowledgment of the universal values we all share as stakeholders in one world with 10,000 cultures.[2] I believe that religion has helped to make these values live in the modern age, as in previous ages, by insisting on their indispensability for all civilizations and cultures. It has already played a vital role within secularism by preserving a sense of the sacred and by encouraging respect for those universally accepted standards of behaviour – not only between individuals but between states – that are now enshrined in the United Nations Charter:[3] standards upholding the inherent dignity of individuals, community rights, and other social or economic or cultural freedoms, duties, and obligations.[4]

---

2 Compare El Hassan bin Talal, "On the Civilisational and Renaissance Project" (University of Jordan, Amman, 14 January 2002).

3 That is, in the Universal Declaration of Human Rights, 1948.

4 Witness, for example, "The Declaration of the Parliament of the World's Religions," in Küng and Kuschel, A Global Ethic, which strives to map a moral ground for human actions. The four basic principles of such an ethic are, in fact, close to the notion of natural right or rights, ius naturalis, and form a minimum common ethical understanding between religions and the cultures adopting these principles.

LIBERAL IDEALS AND ISLAMIC SOCIETIES

Permit me to become a bit more specific by speaking of my own religion, Islam, and of its relation to civil society as we understand it today. The common and vastly distorted picture of Islam is that of a religion that clashes with modern society. As a Muslim, however, I believe that my religion clashes neither with liberalism, nor with pluralism, nor with secularism, nor with democracy. Indeed, Islam has something to contribute to all these concepts and movements, albeit often providing them with an alternative approach. In reply to the notion (recently expounded by Samuel Huntington)[5] that Islam clashes with the civilization of modernity, I have proposed an intra-Muslim dialogue to precede a broader interfaith dialogue. For I would like (in the first instance) to see Muslims reassert the intellectual legacy of the Holy Prophet, his family, and companions through a revisiting of Islam's historic contribution as a preserving and nurturing civilization in its own right. I am certain that we will be surprised by the extent to which those liberal, pluralistic, and democratic values that we so cherish today actually have their roots in religion. And we might be further surprised by the extent to which the notion of representative government, and the idea of society as composed of various autonomous, self-activating groups and associations, is already present within the Islamic tradition itself.[6]

---

5 Huntington, *Clash of Civilizations and the Remaking of World Order.*

6 Traditional Muslim society was ordered around a central political authority, combining temporal and spiritual affairs; but social space was immediately shared by a variety of collective associations wherein civil society included the endowments, the *awqaf* and the guilds, Ulama and merchants, Muslim and non-Muslim sects, and tribes. They ran most of their own internal affairs through elected or appointed leaders, elders, and notables, known as *Ahlu al-Hal wa al-Akd*, or the Solvers and Binders. Indeed, the concept and function of *waqf* and *zakat* provide efficient mechanisms for addressing many difficult aspects of our modern world.

Though autocracy and a stifled intellectualism are perceived by some to be the dominant tendencies of the Islamic world today, Muslim countries do not lack the ability to achieve more inclusive political processes, as countries so far apart as Indonesia and Jordan have already demonstrated. These countries, among others, show that at the grassroots of Muslim culture democracy and the instruments of civil society are thriving. Democratization and transparent, accountable governmental practices are beginning to take hold again in many places. Islamic civil society may be composed of non-governmental organizations (NGOs), trading and banking partnerships, hospitals, charitable foundations, educational institutions, human rights movements, minority communities, think-tanks, and so forth. The ancient role of the guilds is especially noteworthy in having provided not only business links but also various opportunities to undertake charitable donorship, patronage, and social security programs. We also find inspirational examples of active civil society in very recent establishments such as the Grameen Bank, which originated in Bangladesh, and the Katchi Abadis housing projects in Pakistan.

Civil society represents two ideals: (1) the right of each citizen to interact with a representative and accountable government, and (2) the establishment of a set of rules governing the relation between civil society and the state (as well as behaviour within civil society itself). Lack of democracy based on political pluralism, extremist ideology seeking to undermine the rule of law, the resurgence of nationalism and state-sponsored international terrorism are interrelated challenges to civil society that need to be addressed by a new culture of compliance with international mores and norms. Laith Kubba argues that the Islamic principles of freedom, human dignity, equality, governance by contract, popular sovereignty, and the rule of law may not be altogether identical to the cognate principles that belong to the intellectual heritage of liberal democracy, but they are certainly compatible with it.[7] Bernard

---

7 See Laith Kubba, "Islam and Liberal Democracy: Recognizing Pluralism," *Journal of Democracy* 7, 2 (1996): 86–9. Democracy, of

Lewis also acknowledges that there are elements in the Islamic tradition that are not hostile to democracy and that could even help in its development, such as the classical Islamic concept of supreme sovereignty – elective, contractual, consensual, and revocable. Of far greater importance, though, is the acceptance of pluralism in Islamic law and practice, illustrated by Islamic civilization's "astonishing diversity" from the very beginning of its rule.[8]

Here it is interesting to note that Imam Zayn al-Abidin, great grandson of the Holy Prophet, wrote a book of rights, *Kitab al-Huqooq*,[9] which preceded the Charter of Human Rights by many centuries. The earliest practical illustration of the liberality of Islamic principles, however, is a document known as the Constitution of Medina, which articulated agreements concluded between the Prophet Muhammad and the non-Muslim tribes of Medina.[10] The Constitution enabled each party to keep its own laws and customs, and conferred

---

course, as the *2000 Human Development Report* (UNDP) contends, is not homogeneous. It has several forms, with countries choosing different institutional combinations depending upon their circumstances and needs.

8 Bernard Lewis, "Islam and Liberal Democracy," *Atlantic Monthly*, February 1993. In this connection see also Charles Taylor, "Democratic Exclusion (and Its Remedies?)," in Cairns et al. *Citizenship, Diversity and Pluralism.* Professor Taylor, who describes democracy as "a great philosophy of inclusion," nevertheless contends that there is something in the dynamic of democracy that pushes to exclusion because the democratic age opens a new set of issues around the vexing question of political identity vis-à-vis the state. He contrasts this propensity towards exclusionism to the apparent inclusionism of the early Muslim conquerors who, for examply, "often had a very good record of 'multicultural' tolerance and coexistence."

9 New York: Tahrike Tarsile Qur'an, 2001.

10 See Soumaya Ghanoushi, "The Origins of Extremism: Theology or Reality?" *Islam* 21 (December 2001): 319–26.

rights and obligations of citizenship among members of the community on the basis of residence rather than religious belief. The Constitution is at bottom a civil code, and a blueprint for Islamic pluralism, that might be viewed as a basis for democracy and the development of civil society, at least in the Muslim world. Abdul Karim Soroush, perhaps the pre-eminent contemporary Islamic reformer, openly advocates democracy for the Muslim world. Professor Soroush points out that to be a true believer one must be free and under no compulsion, while stressing that an Islamic democracy is only legitimate if it has been chosen by the majority, whether Muslim or not.[11] Ray Takeyh adds to the Soroushian appeal by arguing that, in the hands of thoughtful reformers, Islam is not merely a system for connecting humanity to its divine creator but a force for progressive change. Moreover, the Qur'an's mandate that the community be consulted and rulers be held accountable establishes the platform for collective action and democratic participation.[12]

In sum, the Muslim world has always known activities as well as standards of behaviour that are characteristic of civil society, and today too there are credible and accessible mechanisms for citizens and communities to organize themselves according to their interests and to address their views to government. I would suggest that commentators who reject the possibility of civil society and democratization are overlooking a gradual but nonetheless thoroughgoing process of evolution that is changing our region as comprehensively as any revolution, with perhaps more enduring effects. This process has the support of Islamic teaching, which favours equality, respects individual and communal rights of belief and citizenship, and advocates the peaceful management of diversity. Islam has always flourished on the basis of social and cultural pluralism,

---

11 See "The Idea of Democratic Religious Government" in Soroush, *Reason, Freedom and Democracy in Islam.*

12 Ray Takeyh, "God's Will: Iranian Democracy and the Islamic Context," *Middle East Policy* 7, 4 (October 2000): 41–9.

and the diversity of the *Ummah,* or Islamic polity. Its acknowledgment of and respect for diversity has allowed it to grow and to enrich itself over the centuries by drawing on the deep wellspring of human variety, which it continues to do.

We may view this the other way round as well. In a recent BBC interview[13] I said that pluralism is perhaps the only answer to the Balkanization in many parts of our world – that is, to what some paradoxically, if not disturbingly, refer to as "benign" conflicts. I believe that one of the proper aims of pluralism is to help develop an ethic of human solidarity that will move us away from the hegemony of petro-politics, and Euro versus dollar economics, towards empowering the poor and making the sovereignty of the citizen count. That would be a benign form of politics – *anthropolitics* – as opposed to other types of politics driven by narrower pecuniary concerns. Anthropolitics is a politics of humanity, which may draw from the wells of Islam as from those of other major religions and cultures. In Arabic, the language of the Holy Qur'an, do we not speak for a new moral imperative when we refer to *Rab al-Aalameen,* the God of the world(s) and the God of the universe(s)? We are moving towards a universalization and a sharing in our common humanity, within which the concept of compassion (after the concepts of *Tawhid,* or Unity of God, and *Risalah,* or Messengership of the Holy Prophet) is central.

RELIGION AND HUMAN SOLIDARITY

In considering Islamic intellectual and political thought from a historical perspective, I have sought to emphasise not only its relevance to good governance but its potential contribution to an ethic of human solidarity, a theme I have touched upon on many occasions. As a matter of fact, it is difficult to talk about good governance, or about the universalization of values through an infusion of ethics into world affairs, or about an ethic of human solidarity, without acknowledging

13 BBC Radio 4, 10 April 2003

that human life is not only essentially moral but inherently purposeful. And that is where religion (my own and others) enters the equation.

That purposefulness and morality are corollaries is something to which authentic religion draws our attention. In doing so it underpins the development of all human cultures. Sayyed Hossein Nasr, an Iranian scholar based in the United States, has argued that every civilization is created by religion. One might admit, at least, that every nation-state – whether secular, democratic, theocratic, or even atheist – has some semblance of a religious heritage somewhere in its history. This lends further armour to our defence of religion as a key component in any attempt to sustain our civilizations, that is, to understand and appreciate who, what, where, and perhaps even *why* we are.

But to acknowledge the centrality of religion, and its public nature, is not automatically to become a prisoner of history, which has already seen more than its share of religious conflict. As Nasr has said, if the religions can come to understand each other, not just on a formal level but on the level of inner respect for the same fundamental truths of human existence – if they can come to appreciate each other with a respect over and above mere tolerance – then we will already have laid the foundations for true civilizational dialogue.

With that hope in view let us overcome (if need be) our fear of religion, while religious adherents seek to overcome their fears of other religions and, indeed, of the non-religious.[14] As

---

14 Professor Soroush rightly maintains that the basic religious concepts and values (such as truth, justice, humanity, public interest, and so on) are integral to non-religious value systems as well. Making a related, albeit more critical, point, Douglas Farrow (*First Things*, May 2003, 20–3) argues that secularism is properly liberal when it knows itself to be limited and provisional, not when it imagines itself to be neutral about all things religious or metaphysical. (Professor Farrow asks whether secular systems of thought *can* be religiously neutral. I would caution, however, against confusing

moderator of the World Conference on Religion and Peace, I continue to call for a global ethic of human solidarity while promoting solemn respect for the various faiths and their interaction. Together with Drs Hans Küng and Leonard Swidler, I stress that this ethic should rest on principles that emphasize the association between theory and practice; that support commonality, embracing the commitment to "no coercion" while upholding the right to proclaim one's own religion; that take into account the Enlightenment tradition, reconsidering the content of education and ensuring a free flow of information; that encourage fresh appreciations of our own and each other's texts, heritage, and history, developing a framework for disagreement and producing a context for further enquiry – and that require us to accept responsibility for words and action at all levels.[15]

---

neutrality with what we might call "neutralism." Neutralism negates the need to consider the fluid, interconnecting development of human civilization and ideas, offering the common denominator of values as something to be explained in dialectical terms rather than to be explored through cultural diversity.)

15 Additional sources for this chapter include: Robert D. Crane, "Intellectual and Spiritual Jihad: The Ultimate Power against Terrorism," a paper presented to the roundtable entitled "The Role of Muslim Intellectuals in the Wake of the Terrorist Attacks against the United States," AMSS Conference on Religion and Public Life in the Global Epoch (Dearborn, Michigan, 28 October 2001); Khaled Abou El-Fadl, "Islam: Images, Politics, Paradox," in *Islam and the Theology of Power: Middle East Report* 221 (Winter 2001), viewable at <merip.org>; Graham E. Fuller, "The Future of Political Islam," in *Foreign Affairs* 81, 2 (March-April 2002), 48; Furedi, *New Ideology of Imperialism*; bin Talal and Elkann, *Essere Musulmano*; El Hassan bin Talal, "Coming of Age in the Modern Islamic State" (16 August 2002).

2

Freedom of Religion and the Rule of Law

A Canadian Perspective

THE RIGHT HONOURABLE BEVERLEY
MCLACHLIN, PC

Learned in the humanities and the law, René Cassin was a
distinguished jurist, a visionary statesman, a committed sup-
porter of French language and culture, and an advocate and
pioneer in the emerging field of human rights.[1] Cassin's academic interests were international in scope and humanistic in
nature. As a professor at the University of Paris, he published
extensively on a broad range of legal topics, including contracts,
immigration, equality, and human rights.

But Cassin's commitment to justice and the rule of law did
not end at the classroom door, nor was it bound to the pages
of legal journals. As a statesman, Cassin served for fourteen
years as French delegate to the League of Nations. When
Nazism took root in Europe, Cassin fled France and its capit-
ulating regime to join the government-in-exile. He was an
instrumental force in de Gaulle's government, drafting all of
the administration's legal texts, negotiating the Churchill-de
Gaulle accord, and holding such key positions as president of
the Juridical Committee of the Provisional Government.

---

1 This chapter was originally presented by the Chief Justice of
  Canada as the 2002 René Cassin Lecture, on 11 October, at
  McGill University.

Following the end of the Second World War, René Cassin continued both his academic career and his service to civil society. He served in high posts in the French and European judiciary, sitting on the Constitutional Council of France and occupying the office of president of both the Court of Arbitration in The Hague and the European Court of Human Rights at Strasbourg. His commitment to the inherent dignity of all persons assumed an increasingly international character as his inspiring career progressed. He was a founding member of the United Nations Commission on Human Rights and was instrumental, along with John P. Humphrey of McGill University, in drafting the Universal Declaration of Human Rights, approved by the General Assembly in 1948. In December of 1968, René Cassin was awarded the Nobel Peace Prize.

The Universal Declaration of Human Rights, Cassin's crowning achievement, calls for freedom of conscience and religion, including the freedom "to manifest [one's] religion or belief in teaching, practice, worship and observance."[2] In so doing, it recognizes that modern legal systems bear some responsibility for guaranteeing a safe space within society for religious belief and expression to flourish. The Canadian Charter of Rights and Freedoms also reflects a commitment to the state's role in protecting religious freedom. There is little doubt that the Charter has ushered in a new era of protection for religious conscience in Canada. While I do want to address some ways in which the Charter has influenced the protection of religion, I wish to begin by considering some fundamental questions that are engaged by the very inquiry into freedom of religion in a modern state. In so doing, I hope to explore Canada's unique historical experience of protecting religious liberties as well as the role that the law and the courts have played in this endeavour.

---

2 Universal Declaration of Human Rights, G.A. Res. 217 A(III), UN Doc. A/810, at 71 (1948), art. 18.

THE FUNDAMENTAL TENSION

In his work on the cultural study of law, Yale Professor Paul Kahn describes the rule of law as a comprehensive system of belief. "There is no part of modern life," Kahn explains, "to which law does not extend."[3] Kahn is describing the way in which, from the subjective viewpoint of the individual, the rule of law exerts an authoritative claim upon all aspects of selfhood and experience in a liberal democratic society. Some such claims are made by the institutional structures of the law. Others are ancillary claims arising from a diffused ethos of legal rule that influences local, community, and familial structures. The authority claimed by law touches upon all aspects of human life and citizenship. As Kahn writes, "the rule of law shapes our experience of meaning everywhere and at all times. It is not alone in shaping meaning, but it is rarely absent."[4] Voting, taxation, mobility, family organization, and public discourse: the rule of law leaves no aspect of human experience unaffected by its claim to authority.

Many of these claims upon the legal subject flow from a conception of authority rooted in the sovereign, variously conceived of as the Queen, the executive, the Constitution, or the people themselves. The legal significance of the concept of precedent demonstrates that the law also claims authority through the operation of history, finding historical reasons for asserting influence over the modern lives of citizens. But while the rule of law makes total claims upon the self, it is also, in the words of Professor Kahn, "a way of being in the world that must compete with other forms of social and political perception."[5] That is, there are other sources of authority, other cultural modes of belief, that make strong claims upon the citizen.

---

3 *The Cultural Study of Law*, 123.

4 Ibid., 124.

5 Ibid., 84.

The acclaimed cultural anthropologist Clifford Geertz describes religion as one such competing system of belief and cultural belonging. In his classic text, *The Interpretation of Cultures*, Geertz described religion as a cultural form that imbues all facets of the adherent's life and finds authority in transcendent principles. For the religious subject – the adherent – religion's authority touches not only upon beliefs about transcendent aspects of the universe but also affects all aspects of the way the subject moves and orients within the social and political world. As Geertz puts it:

Religion is never merely metaphysics. For all peoples the forms, vehicles, and objects of worship are suffused with an aura of deep moral seriousness. The holy bears within it everywhere a sense of intrinsic obligation: it not only encourages devotion, it demands it; it not only induces intellectual assent, it enforces emotional commitment. Whether it be formulated as *mana*, as *Brahma*, or as the Holy Trinity, that which is set apart as more than mundane is inevitably considered to have far-reaching implications for the direction of human conduct.[6]

As such, in Geertz's terms, religion is both worldview *and* ethos; it affects belief *and* action. There are no limits to the claims made by religion upon the self. Religious authority, grounded as it is in basic assumptions about the nature of the cosmos, impinges upon all aspects of the adherent's world.[7] Indeed, the Supreme Court recognized the pervasive effect of religious belief upon the adherent in *R. v. Edwards Books.*[8] Chief Justice Dickson characterized religion as "profoundly personal beliefs that govern one's perception of oneself, humankind, nature, and, in some cases, a higher or different

---

6 *The Interpretation of Cultures*, 126.

7 See also Eliade, *The Sacred and the Profane*, 167ff.

8 [1986] 2 S.C.R. 713.

order of being. These beliefs, in turn, govern one's conduct and practices."[9]

These overarching demands of the rule of law and of religious conscience dramatize one of the foundational issues raised by the legal protection of freedom of religion. As Dicey explained, a fundamental tenet of the rule of law is that all people are subject to its authority. It makes total claims upon the self and leaves little of human experience untouched. Yet religion exerts a similarly comprehensive claim. In the minds of adherents, its authority stands outside and above that of the law. So by examining freedom of religion, we are asking how one authoritative and ubiquitous system of cultural understanding – the rule of law – accommodates another similarly comprehensive system of belief. The modern religious citizen is caught between two all-encompassing sets of commitments. The law faces the seemingly paradoxical task of asserting its own ultimate authority while carving out a space within itself in which individuals and communities can manifest alternate, and often competing, sets of ultimate commitments.

THE CANADIAN EXPERIENCE

The uniquely Canadian experience of the legal protection of religious conscience is that from the outset – even before the creation of Canada as an autonomous nation – the law has been charged with the responsibility for creating this space. For Canada, religious liberty under the law is not an issue that emerged as the state matured; rather, it is an issue that has been at play since the country's inception, has been a topic for judicial consideration, and has since been entrenched in our fundamental laws. Canadian law has always been concerned in some manner with freedom of religion, and the courts have, therefore, always been a forum in which these issues have been deliberated.

9 Ibid., 759.

One can trace the issue of religious liberty in Canada to the articles of capitulation for Quebec and Montreal in 1759 and 1760, respectively. Both documents granted the inhabitants of the cities "the free exercise of the roman religion."[10] Despite the Crown's desire to extend the Church of England to the New World, the Treaty of Paris, which formally recognized Britain's claim to Canada in 1763, included a provision that guaranteed the rights of Roman Catholics to practise their religion in Canada. The British King promised to "give the most express and the most effectual orders that his new Roman Catholic subjects may profess the worship of their religion according to the rights of the Romish church, as far as the laws of Great Britain permit."[11] This final proviso – "as far as the laws of Great Britain permit" – threatened to eviscerate the guarantee: English penal laws of the time effectively banned Roman Catholicism, including the sacrament of the mass. However a legal opinion of the Attorney and Solicitor Generals issued in 1765 declared that Roman Catholics living in Canada were not subject to the penal laws of England.[12] This exemption guaranteed the freedom to practise a religion not condoned by the state.

The Quebec Act, 1774, gave fuller articulation to this approach to freedom of religion, providing that Roman Catholic residents of Quebec were entitled to the free exercise of religion, while the Crown was simultaneously empowered to encourage the Protestant religion and support the Protestant clergy.[13] An even more expansive concept of religious liberty was set out in an 1851 statute that guaranteed to all Canadians "the free exercise and enjoyment of Religious Profession and

---

10 Art. VI of the Articles of Capitulation of Quebec, in Shortt and
   Doughty, *Documents Relating to the Constitutional History of Canada,*
   1759–1791, 6. See also Art. XVI of the Articles of Capitulation for
   Montreal (ibid., 25).
11 Ibid., 89.
12 Ibid., 171.
13 14 George III, c. 83.

Worship, without discrimination or preference."[14] This same statute asserted that "the recognition of legal equality among all Religious Denominations is an admitted principle of Colonial Legislation," that Canada was a province "to which such a principle is peculiarly applicable," and that this notion of the legal protection of religion is "a fundamental principle of our civil polity."[15] Ultimately, with Confederation, the British North America Act, 1867, introduced a constitutional guarantee for minority religious schools, a guarantee of continuing legal significance.[16] Thus, the Canadian experience of legally recognized religious liberty was forged in the laws of the country. These were the early legislative pronouncements on the need to accommodate religious diversity within the rule of law. But, ultimately, similar overarching principles were independently recognized in decisions of the courts.

There is a breadth of historical case law invoking various legal mechanisms to guarantee a space for religious commitments within the rule of law. In *Re Drummond Wren*, a 1945 decision of the Ontario High Court,[17] the court was faced with reconciling the general legal acceptance of an owner's ability to alienate land as he sees fit with a restrictive covenant that provided that particular property was "not to be sold to Jews." Justice Keiller MacKay was provided with a set of bases upon which he could find the restrictive covenant invalid: that it was an undue restraint on alienation, that it was void for uncertainty, and that it contravened the provisions of Ontario's Racial Discrimination Act, 1944. Yet Justice MacKay found that it was not necessary to resort to any of these more narrow legal mechanisms; rather, the covenant was void as contravening "public policy." Justice MacKay appealed to international recognition of freedom of religion and found the covenant invalid for the following reasons: "the consequences of judicial

---

14 14 and 15 Victoria, c. 175.

15 Ibid.

16 *British North America Act, 1867* (UK), 30 and 31 Victoria, c. 3, s. 93.

17 [1945] 4 D.L.R. 674 (Ont. H.C.) (*"Drummond Wren"*).

approbation of such a covenant are portentous. If sale of a piece of land can be prohibited to Jews, it can equally be prohibited to Protestants, Catholics or other groups or denominations. If the sale of one piece of land can be so prohibited, the sale of other pieces of land can likewise be prohibited. In my opinion, nothing could be more calculated to create or deepen divisions between existing religious and ethnic groups in this Province, or in this country."[18] The freedom of commercial transactions had to give way to the need for the law to create a space for religious conscience. In this case, it was the courts, drawing upon diffuse notions of public policy, that carved out this space.

The Supreme Court of Canada effected a similar result, albeit in a very different context, in *Chaput v. Romain et al.*[19] Members of the Quebec provincial police force broke up an orderly religious meeting of Jehovah's Witnesses. The police stopped the service, seized a Bible and other religious texts, and ordered the participants to disperse. Although the officers were acting on instructions from their superiors – and the implication was that these orders reflected the wishes of the community – the entire court held that they had no right to interfere with this religious practice. Justice Taschereau, who authored the plurality reasons, forcefully stated the principle that all religions are entitled to equal respect under the law:

Dans notre pays, il n'existe pas de religion d'État. Personne n'est tenu d'adhérer à une croyance quelconque. Toutes les religions sont sur un pied d'égalité, et tous les catholiques comme d'ailleurs tous les protestants, les juifs ou les autres adhérents des diverses dénominations religieuses, ont la plus entière liberté de penser comme ils le désirent. La conscience de chacun est une affaire personnelle, et l'affaire de nul autre. Il serait désolant de penser qu'une majorité puisse imposer ses vues religieuses à une minorité. Ce serait une erreur fâcheuse de croire qu'on sert son pays ou sa religion, en

---

18 Ibid., 678.

19 [1955] S.C.R. 834 (*"Chaput"*).

refusant dans une province, à une minorité, les mêmes droits que l'on revendique soi-même avec raison, dans une autre province.[20]

What was the precedent for this pronouncement? What enshrined statement of rights or supreme articulation of law authorized this statement? Justice Taschereau did not rely upon legislative pronouncement. He was articulating principles indigenous to the legal order in Canada: the rule of law must incorporate within itself some space for the manifestation of religious conscience. The decision in *Chaput* merely instantiated this amorphous concept in a particular case.

These two cases, *Drummond Wren* and *Chaput*, are examples drawn from a body of jurisprudence that demonstrates the abiding Canadian legal commitment to religious freedom within the rule of law. While neither invokes a particular statute guaranteeing religious liberty, both appeal to principles that subtend Canada's legal system. Both also reflect the fact that the courts have maintained an enduring responsibility for finding, in the comprehensive claims of the rule of law, a space in which individual and community adherence to religious authority can flourish.

In the twentieth century, the Canadian Bill of Rights,[21] human rights documents, and the Charter of Rights and Freedoms[22] have served as the main legal articulations of Canada's commitment to religious freedom. But the foregoing demonstrates that the question of finding a place for religious conscience in a liberal polity has been a thread running through the whole fabric of Canadian legal and political history. As Justice Rand stated in *Samur v. Quebec (City)*,[23] "[f]rom

---

20 Ibid., 840.

21 S.C. 1960, c. 44, s. 1(c).

22 *Canadian Charter of Rights and Freedoms*, Part I of the *Constitution Act, 1982*, being Schedule B to the *Canada Act 1982* (UK), 1982, c. 11.

23 [1953] 2 S.C.R. 299.

1760 ... to the present moment religious freedom has, in our legal system, been recognized as a principle of fundamental character."[24] It is a question among those at the foundation of Canadian legal life, and one that has persisted in both subsequent legislation and case law. The law has always assumed the central role of reconciling the overarching need for adherence to the rule of law with respect for religious commitments to systems of belief and authority, some of which are profoundly extra-legal in nature. When we inquire into religious freedoms in Canada, therefore, we are exploring one aspect of a theme that suffuses Canadian legal history – the challenge that the law faces when it takes religious freedom seriously.

THE CLASH OF COMMITMENTS

Religious worldviews, both consonant and dissonant with the authority of the state, have always been the topic of legislation and legal consideration in Canada. Equally, the synthesis of the rule of law with seemingly contradictory religious belief systems has always been a matter for the courts. Case law has not been limited to the protection of minority interests; it has included those cases in which the sources of authority and content of religious conscience actually clash with the prevailing ethos of the rule of law. I wish to call this tension between the rule of law and the claims of religion a "dialectic of normative commitments." What is good, true, and just in religion will not always comport with the law's view of the matter, nor will society at large always properly respect conscientious adherence to alternate authorities and divergent normative, or ethical, commitments. Where this is so, two comprehensive worldviews collide. It is at this point that the question of law's treatment of religion becomes truly exigent. The authority of each is internally unassailable. What is more, both lay some claim to the whole of human experience. To which system should

---

24 Ibid., 327.

the subject adhere? How can the rule of law accommodate a
worldview and ethos that asserts its own superior authority and
unbounded scope? There seems to be no way in which to reconcile this clash; yet these clashes do occur in a society dedicated to protecting religion, and a liberal state must find some
way of reconciling these competing commitments.

It is the courts that are most often faced with this clash and
charged with managing this dialectic. While the guarantee of
freedom of religion is introduced into the legal landscape by
legislators, this is only one aspect of giving content to the
protection. The struggle faced by the courts is one of balancing. On the one hand stands society's need for adherence to
the rule of law. The rule of law presents itself as an authoritative force and, in a democracy, the content of this authority
generally reflects majoritarian views and interests. For society
to function properly it must be able to depend on some general consensus with respect to the norms that should be manifested in the law. The authority of the rule of law depends
upon this. On the other hand, in Canadian society there is
the value that we place upon multiculturalism and diversity,
which brings with it a commitment to freedom of religion.
But the beliefs and actions manifested when this freedom is
granted can collide with conventional legal norms. This clash
of forces demands a resolution from the courts. The reality
of litigation means that cases must be resolved. The dialectic
must reach synthesis.

So the courts struggle to oversee those points in public life
where there is a clash between religious conscience and society's values as manifested in the rule of law. A space for minority religious expression must be created, but this has to be
achieved without compromising core areas of our civil commitments. This task is made even more formidable because it
often requires a balancing of values that are independently
fundamental to the polity. To name just two examples: individual autonomy, on the one hand, and community integrity
on the other; or anti-discrimination *versus* respect for conscientious belief. Cases drawn from the jurisprudence can help
to illustrate the challenge of this role.

A fascinating 1970 case from the Supreme Court of Canada, *Hofer v. Interlake Colony of Hutterian Brethren*,[25] effectively conveys the complexity of managing this dialectic of normative commitments. The appellants and respondents were members of the Interlake Hutterite Colony. A fundamental Hutterite belief involves the commitment to communal ownership of property. The appellants were a small group within the community whose religious beliefs on topics such as property holding and communal authority shifted away from those of the majority. The Colony's Articles of Association contained a provision for the expulsion of members, and the appellants were expelled from the colony. The expelled parties brought an action seeking, among other things, a declaration that they were still part of the colony and a division of the colony's assets among all of the members. The respondents counter-claimed, asking for a declaration that the appellants had been properly expelled, were no longer entitled to share in the property, had to return their personal property, and vacate the colony's land. The courts below held that the appellants were properly expelled and had no claim to the property in question. The Supreme Court of Canada agreed.

While the case was fundamentally decided on principles of fairness in decision making, one of the arguments marshalled by the appellants was that the church authorities' unlimited power and control over both the personal lives of members and of the colony's communal property was contrary to public policy. On this question, Chief Justice Cartwright reasoned that the expelled parties had entered into the agreement that formed the normative foundation for the community. Unless such contracts were held to be valid, "it is difficult to see how the Hutterian Brethren could carry on the form of religious life which they believe to be the right one."[26] There can be

---

25 [1970] S.C.R. 958 (*"Hofer"*). For another religious freedom case from this time touching upon Hutterite beliefs, see *Walter v. A.G. Alta.; Fletcher v. A.G. Alta.*, [1969] S.C.R. 383.

26 Ibid., 963.

little doubt that the tenets of the Hutterite faith, including communal living and ownership of property, conflicted with the prevailing legal norms of the time. Indeed, autonomy of decision making and free property holding remain important aspects of the rule of law. But Chief Justice Cartwright was able to find space for these religious practices within the rule of law. In this space, the colony would be able to manifest its religious conscience without impinging unduly on either the core values of society or the rights and freedoms of others. This balancing is even more starkly evident in Justice Ritchie's reasons for the plurality: "There is no doubt that the Hutterian way of life is not that of the vast majority of Canadians, but it makes manifest a form of religious philosophy to which any Canadian can subscribe and it appears to me that if any individual either through birth within the community or by choice wishes to subscribe to such a rigid form of life and to subject himself to the harsh disciplines of the Hutterian Church, he is free to do so."[27] This reasoning reflects the careful balancing of the demands of the rule of law with the exigencies of religious conscience – a balancing process characteristic of Canadian courts' role in managing the complex interplay between the authority of the rule of law and the authoritative claims of religion.

A more modern case illustrates the same struggle to find space for religious conscience amidst the values and demands of the rule of law. In 1990, in a case called *Malette v. Shulman*,[28] the Ontario Court of Appeal held that a capable adult Jehovah's Witness who objected to blood transfusions on religious grounds was entitled to withhold consent, even if her life would be put in jeopardy as a result. Although this decision centred on a tort claim of battery, the court recognized that it was a case involving competing fundamental values. The state's interest in preserving life conflicted with the value of personal autonomy, here engaged by Ms. Malette's religiously

---

27 Ibid., 974f.
28 (1990) 72 O.R. (2d) 417 (C.A.) ("*Malette*").

informed refusal to consent to treatment. On balance, the interest in preserving autonomy over one's own body, motivated by whatever ethic, was deemed paramount. The issue was somewhat more involved when, five years later, the Supreme Court considered *R.B. v. Children's Aid Society of Metropolitan Toronto*.[29] In this case, Jehovah's Witness parents refused to consent to a blood transfusion for their infant daughter, a transfusion that might prove necessary to save the child's life. The state assumed wardship of the daughter and the parents challenged the legality of this decision. As such, the case placed the issue of freedom of religion in a clash with the state's interest in preserving the lives of the vulnerable.

In a decision written by Justice LaForest, the court concluded that the state's intervention was justifiable. The court recognized that, like choices about education, "the right of parents to rear their children according to their religious beliefs, including that of choosing medical and other treatment, is an equally fundamental aspect of freedom of religion."[30] In this way, the court acknowledged that religious conscience makes a total claim upon the ethics of the believer and, as such, decisions about how to care for children generally deserve the protection of the law. Yet the court also stated that "freedom of religion is not absolute"[31] and that, in the circumstances of this case, the law's concern for protection of the child, and the child's rights, justified the state's actions.

There are a host of other cases that evidence the courts' role in synthesizing conflicts between and among normative commitments. *Zylberberg v. Sudbury Board of Education*[32] and other cases on issues relating to education, along with *Young v. Young*[33]

---

29 [1995] 1 S.C.R. 315 ("*R.B.*").
30 Ibid., par. 105.
31 Ibid., par. 107.
32 (1988) 52 D.L.R. 577 (Ont. C.A.).
33 [1993] 4 S.C.R. 3.

and the post-Charter line of Sunday-closing cases,[34] are all demonstrative of this task and show that decisions are not easy where the demands of religious conscience conflict with the fundamental values of the rule of law.

However, the case law also shows that the challenges facing the law have not always been met in ways that accord with our current sense of balance. There have been dark points in the courts' management of this dialectic of normative commitments. One example arises from the pre-Charter Sunday-closing case, *R. v. Robertson and Rosetanni*.[35] This case, argued under the Bill of Rights, concerned two proprietors who were convicted of operating their bowling alley on a Sunday, contrary to the Lord's Day Act.[36] The appellants argued that freedom of religion included the freedom to practise one's own religion without being confined by restrictions of Parliament that reflect the tenets of another faith. The court did not agree. Rather, Justice Ritchie chose to look at the effects of the legislation, not the purpose, and could "see nothing in that statute which in any way affects the liberty of religious thought and practice of any citizen of this country."[37] The court held that the detriment suffered by the appellants, rather than infringing their religious freedom, was "a purely secular and financial one in that they are required to refrain from carrying on or conducting their business on Sunday as well as on their own day of rest."[38]

Subsequent case law has demonstrated that this court no longer accepts the position articulated by Justice Ritchie. But even at the time, Justice Cartwright expressed a prescient dissent, stating simply that "a law which compels a course of

---

34 *R. v. Big M. Drug Mart Ltd.*, [1985] 1 S.C.R. 295 (*"Big M."*) and *R. v. Edwards Books and Art Ltd.*, [1986] 2 S.C.R. 713 (*"Edwards Books"*).

35 [1963] S.C.R. 651 (*"Robertson and Rosetanni"*).

36 R.S.C. 1952, c. 171.

37 Ibid., 657.

38 Ibid., 657f.

conduct, whether positive or negative, for a purely religious purpose infringes the freedom of religion."[39]

The history of Doukhobor strife with the state over the issue of education provides another example of Canadian courts reaching unfortunate results when attempting to reconcile clashing normative commitments.[40] The Doukhobor community in British Columbia objected on religious grounds to their children being educated by the public schools. As Professor McLaren notes, they "possessed a hostility toward, or at least profound distrust of, government and the exercise of state power and felt a strong commitment to put God before earthly authority."[41] The state felt the need to intervene and committed the Doukhobor children to the superintendent of child welfare in order to enforce the education scheme. In *Perepolkin v. Superintendent of Child Welfare*[42] a five-member panel of the British Columbia Court of Appeal considered whether the removal of the children from the parents' care was a legal intervention in the lives of these Doukhobor families. The appellants claimed that the sections of the school act permitting the state to so intervene offended their freedom of religion. Justice Sidney Smith, with whom the majority of the court agreed on this point, refused to accept that "in this case there is any religious element involved in the true legal sense. It seems to me that religion is one thing; a code of ethics another; a code of manners, another."[43] Presumably, he viewed the choice about how to educate one's children as an ethical, rather than a religious, decision. As such, the court held that these Doukhobors did not have a right to conscientiously

---

39 Ibid., 660.

40 For a contextual discussion of the Doukhobor experience of land issues, see J. McLaren, "The Doukhobor Belief in Individual Faith and Conscience and the Demands of the Secular State," in McLaren and Coward, eds., *Religious Conscience, the State, and the Law,* 128.

41 McLaren, 121.

42 (1957) 11 D.L.R. (2d) 417 (B.C.C.A.) ("*Perepolkin*").

43 Ibid., 423.

object to the manner of their children's education. Of course, the Supreme Court of Canada has since, in *R.B.*, affirmed that the choices that parents make as to their children's education are an important facet of freedom of religion.

Although we might now take legal and moral exception to these examples from darker points in the history of Canadian courts' treatment of religious liberty, all of the cases cited above, irrespective of the result, are demonstrative of the struggle at the core of the courts' treatment of religious freedom within the rule of law. Conscientiously held religious beliefs and the resulting religious practices can come into conflict with values reflected in the law as a whole. In such cases, the rule of law – itself an all-encompassing authoritative system of cultural understanding – faces practices and beliefs sourced in a wholly extra-legal authority. The value of freedom of religion is, in these instances, in tension with parallel values of critical moment in the society at large. As the Supreme Court recently articulated in *T.W.U.*,[44] in such cases, "any potential conflict should be resolved through the proper delineation of the rights and values involved."[45] The challenge faced by the courts when attempting to find space within the rule of law for diverse expressions of religious conscience is, therefore, one of balancing competing cultural values. Due recognition must be given to the dignity of individuals and communities bound by a religious worldview and ethos, but this must be done without compromising the integrity of the rule of law and the values for which it stands.

WHAT IS THE CONTRIBUTION OF THE CHARTER OF RIGHTS AND FREEDOMS?

A central thesis of this chapter has been that the Canadian experience of religious freedoms has placed the courts in the

---

44 *Trinity Western University v. British Columbia College of Teachers*, [2001] 1 S.C.R. 772 ("*T.W.U.*").

45 Ibid., par. 29.

unique position of managing a dialectic of normative commitments. This dialectic involves balancing the comprehensive
claims of the rule of law with individual and community adherence to worldviews and ethical systems wholly extra-legal in
nature. The courts are, in effect, called upon to carve out a
space within the rule of law in which religious commitments
and claims to authority – sometimes wholly at odds with legal
values and authority – can manifest and flourish. While I have
briefly explored the historical roots of this dialectic and have
canvassed case law demonstrating the role that the courts are
called upon to assume, the modern legal picture of religious
freedoms cannot be complete without giving attention to the
impact of the Charter of Rights and Freedoms.

As demonstrated above, the Charter did not introduce the
concept of religious freedom into the Canadian legal landscape. On the contrary, notions of religious liberty reach back
to pre-Confederation times and suffuse legislation and case
law since that time. What, then, has been the impact of the
Charter? The answers are manifold, but I want to focus upon
one aspect of the Charter's contribution to the dialectic of
normative commitments – the linguistic contribution.

Charles Taylor has contributed greatly to our understanding
of the way in which individuals and communities situate themselves in society and ascribe meaning to their actions and
experiences. In the opening chapter of his most ambitious
work, *Sources of the Self*, Professor Taylor develops his thesis that
people are always acting and finding meaning in a normative
context. He argues that we orient ourselves towards the good
based on our evaluation of what is incomparably crucial to
being human. The good, therefore, forms the horizon, or the
framework, in which we take a stance with respect to "good
human living" and, as a corollary, "a good and just society."
While Professor Taylor is speaking in this volume of individual
identity, I think that our understanding of the dynamics of
community and societal identity are equally enriched by his
observations: "My identity is defined by the commitments and
identifications which provide the frame or horizon within
which I can try to determine from case to case what is good,

or valuable, or what ought to be done, or what I endorse or
oppose. In other words, it is the horizon within which I am
capable of taking a stand."[46] But Taylor also argues that not
all goods are created equal. Some goods, what he calls "hypergoods," are those from which all other normative positions are
judged. They are the basic elements of our normative commitments and exist as "markers" in our horizon of meaning.

How, then, do we become aware of the hypergoods in our
horizons of meaning? Taylor here argues for the centrality of
articulation – the need to put our understandings of the good
into language so that they can affect our lives and choices.
Words have the effect of bringing into conscious awareness
the values by which we guide our actions and interpret our
world. When brought into explicit awareness, our appraisals
of the good are available for evaluation in light of the context,
social or personal, in which we find ourselves. Articulating our
hypergoods is also, in Taylor's scheme, "a necessary condition
of adhesion."[47] That is, by casting our normative commitments
in language, we ensure that these goods remain contiguous
with and relevant to our lives and decisions. Articulation,
then, brings our implicit values to the foreground and makes
them available for both application and debate. As Taylor
writes: "a formulation has power when it brings the source
close, when it makes it plain and evident, in all its inherent
force, its capacity to inspire our love, respect, or allegiance.
An effective articulation releases this force, and this is how
words have power."[48]

This theoretical backdrop highlights one facet of the
Charter's impact upon the concept of religious freedom. The
significance of affording freedom of conscience and religion
a privileged position as part of the supreme law of Canada
cannot be overlooked. However, it is arguable that the Charter
was equally important because of its role in articulating the

---

46 *Sources of the Self* (Cambridge: Harvard University Press, 1989), 27.
47 Ibid., 91.
48 Ibid., 96.

core values – or hypergoods – in our society. There can be no doubt that the Charter's linguistic contribution has, indeed, resulted in adhesion in the sense that Taylor describes. Once articulated in the Charter, freedom of religion cannot help but remain contiguous with the life of our society. The Charter has articulated freedom of religion as one of our society's goods, along with parallel goods guaranteed in other sections. But in addition, case law interpreting the Charter has contributed to and refined this articulation, helping us to understand what we mean by "religious freedom" and what values it protects. In this sense, the Charter awakened a discussion about the purposes and objectives of protecting religious freedom and, in so doing, called upon us all to better articulate our normative commitments.

What, then, is the result of this discussion of the values protected by religious freedom? What hypergoods have been drawn into high-relief? Cast in Taylor's language, what has the Charter revealed to be "incomparably crucial to being human" in our society?

One set of answers has come from the courts, and the touchstone lies with former Chief Justice Dickson's reasons in *R. v. Big M. Drug Mart Ltd.* He undertook a careful examination of the origins of the protection of religious freedom and concluded that, "in this context, the purpose of freedom of conscience and religion becomes clear." Justice Dickson stated that the values "that underlie our political and philosophic traditions demand that every individual be free to hold and to manifest whatever beliefs and opinions his or her conscience dictates, provided *inter alia* only that such manifestations do not injure his or her neighbours or their parallel rights to hold and manifest beliefs and opinions of their own."[49] Freedom of religion, in this view, counsels both for the absence of coercion and respect for diversity of opinions. In *Big M.*, the court asserted that this need for freedom and diversity lay at the core of our society:

---

49 *Big M.*, 346.

A truly free society is one which can accommodate a wide variety of
beliefs, diversity of tastes and pursuits, customs and codes of conduct.
A free society is one which aims at equality with respect to the enjoyment of fundamental freedoms and I say this without reliance upon
s. 15 of the *Charter*. Freedom must surely be founded in respect for
the inherent dignity and the inviolable rights of the human person.[50]

This description of religious freedom fits well with Taylor's
notion of articulating normative goods. The court is effectively
placing markers in society's horizon of meaning, explaining
what values are incomparably crucial to Canadian society.
According to Justice Dickson, these values include human dignity, autonomy, and respect for the parallel rights of others.

Judicial considerations since *Big M.,* including some of
those discussed above, have frequently returned to this statement of principle and have applied these ideas to various fac-
tual situations. Yet, as the legal pluralists have taught us, the
official law and legal institutions of the state are not the only
source of views about law that matter in society.[51] Legal ideas
are generated within, and circulate throughout, all kinds of
societal institutions and take on meanings and bearings germane to those contexts.[52] The Charter has affected the way in
which family units, classrooms, and, most important for the
purposes of this discussion, religious communities have talked
about the import and purpose of religious liberties. Alongside
the doctrinal law as delineated by the court, the language of
dignity, freedom, autonomy, and rights has permeated all

50 Ibid., 336.

51 See, for example, M. Kleinhaus and R.A. Macdonald, "What Is
   Critical Legal Pluralism?" *Canadian Journal of Law and Society* 12
   (1998): 25; and S. Van Praagh, "The Chutzpah of Chasidism,"
   Canadian Journal of Law and Society 11 (1996): 193.

52 As B. De Sousa Santos has noted, "we live in a time of porous
   legality or of legal porosity" ("Law: A Map of Misreading. Toward
   a Postmodern Conception of Law," *Journal of Law and Society* 14
   [1987]: 298).

aspects of the public sphere; and each of these conversations about freedom of religion impinges upon the next. Casting all of this back into Charles Taylor's theoretical framework, the Charter has articulated and laid bare, for discussion and application, both the good of religious freedom and the hypergoods, the core values, it reflects.

CONCLUSION

This chapter has explored the central tensions involved when religious conscience and the rule of law meet in a modern liberal democracy. I have used the language of "dialectic," "conflict," and "clash" to emphasize the struggles faced when trying to create a space within the rule of law in which religious beliefs and practices can manifest. But I want to conclude by emphasizing another aspect of the relationship between Canadian law and religion, one that focuses on the product of the legal and social path that this country has travelled.

Over the past 250 years, the issue of religious freedom has matured alongside the growing diversity of the country. The days of the Treaty of Paris have passed and the law is no longer solely concerned with striking the right balance between the Church of England and Roman Catholicism. We have all come to understand that there were religions in this country before either of these traditions took root and that the people that have since become part of the Canadian mosaic have introduced innumerable other faith perspectives. As the cultural diversity of our nation has developed, I think we have come to recognize that a multiplicity of worldviews grounded in alternative sources of authority does not necessarily threaten the rule of law but, rather, strengthens and completes public life and discourse. Even more critically, we have come to a fuller appreciation of the intrinsic connection between respecting religious conscience and attending to the inherent dignity of all persons. Freedom of conscience and religion has become a component of the Canadian experience of the rule of law.

In this respect, I believe that the law has matured along with society. As I have tried to demonstrate in this chapter, the

challenges for the courts are formidable in this area. But the
law is tenacious and has a tremendous capacity to meet the
challenges that society presents. Canada's experience of freedom of religion is a particularly rich one. The courts have an
abiding responsibility to draw upon this history and thereby
cultivate the law's ability to give meaning to religious freedom
while maintaining our highest civic commitments.

A Response
to Chief Justice McLachlin

JEAN BETHKE ELSHTAIN

It is indeed an honour to respond to the Right Honourable Chief Justice. I learned a great deal reading her paper.* What I will bring to these brief reflections is a sensibility honed in a country, the United States, whose point of origin is inseparable from political liberty and the free exercise of religion; in a time, the immediate post-Second World War era, when one of the monstrous totalitarianisms of the twentieth century lay in ruins and the West, led by the United States, was engaged in a long, twilight struggle against the second; and in a faith, Christianity, that turns on the belief that human beings are created in God's image and are, therefore, of inestimable worth – a faith that therefore speaks readily and gladly, with the Chief Justice, of the "inherent dignity of all persons."[1]

With that, I move directly to my comments. The Right Honourable Chief Justice begins with what she calls "the fundamental tension" between the comprehensive, authoritative, and total claims of both law and religion. Given that the writ of each extends to all aspects of human life – making "total claims upon the self" (here her characterization of law but

---

* Editor's note: This response was given orally on the occasion of the 2002 René Cassin lecture.

1 Pope John Paul II urges that, when one sees before one a fellow human being, one is obliged to pause at the irreducible.

the same holds for religion) – clashes are bound to occur. She sets the stage for such clashes with her claim that law and religion are equally total and comprehensive worldviews. But one of them, the law, is assigned the task of "accommodating" the other.

I will begin by querying this way of characterizing the question before us as the framing of the question looks a bit different if one abstains from a strong version of comprehensive claims for the law. Surely, where the rule of law in the West is concerned, there is a great deal about which the law is simply silent: the "King's writ" does not extend to every nook and cranny. Indeed, a great deal of self-governing autonomy and authority is not only permitted but is necessary to a pluralistic, constitutional order characterized by limited government. In other words, the law need not be defined as total and comprehensive in the way the Right Honourable Chief Justice claims.

But what of religion? Surely *it* exempts nothing. Not so fast. Religion, in social worlds in which it is virtually coterminous with culture itself, can certainly be said to be total and comprehensive. But in the formation of Western culture and politics there was that fateful moment when Jesus of Nazareth examined a coin: "Render unto Caesar what is Caesar's; unto God what is God's." Over time, this evolved into a strong view of the relative autonomy of the governmental order, for it, too, is mandated by God and it, too, makes legitimate claims on us.

Where the line is to be drawn – where Caesar illegitimately usurps what is God's – varies from one religious tradition or denomination to another. And from the side of religion might come usurpation, too. Faith may usurp what is properly within the legitimate mandate of government. However, given the power and reach of the modern state, the encroachment by one into the mandate of the other is more likely to flow from structures of governmental power, at least in the West, which has never been hospitable to theocracy. Close alliances between throne and altar are not the same thing, not at all. The corollary to the relative autonomy of government is the autonomy of faith. Law is enjoined to recognize the space that faith occupies. A good bit of the history of the West is a story of the ongoing struggle over what we now routinely call church and state, and their respective purviews.[2]

Now let us consider the way in which one might tell this story against a bit of the backdrop that we should pause for a moment to recall: the terms of the modern regime of religious toleration. More specifically, let us remind ourselves of the contours of the argument in John Locke's justly famous *Letter on Toleration.* Locke drew up a map with religion cast as soul-craft, government as statescraft. A person could be a citizen of each so long as religion meant primarily freedom of conscience and belief rather than strong institutional loyalty to a religious body that engaged the society in all its aspects. Locke, remember, said that all religions save atheism and Roman Catholicism were to be tolerated. Atheists couldn't be tolerated as they would not take an oath on the Bible, and Catholics did not fit within the terms of the tolerance regime because they had a double loyalty: they were loyal to a strong church. It was the institutional presence and authority of the Roman Catholic Church that seemed to unhinge Locke on this question. In the words of one of the United States' leading constitutional scholars of the free exercise of religion, Michael McConnell: "Locke's exclusion of atheists and Catholics from toleration cannot be dismissed as a quaint exception to his beneficent liberalism; it follows logically from the ground on which his argument for toleration rested." But, as McConnell adds, if religious freedom means "nothing more than that religion should be free so long as it is irrelevant to the state, it does not mean very much."[3]

---

2 One upshot of these struggles is that, at present, to trigger open defiance and disobedience of law from the side of the vast majority of religious believers, the provocation must be quite substantial. Dissent and disagreement – the stuff of democratic politics, after all – are far more common, of course, since so many political questions are also ethical questions and impinge on matters of faith, even as matters of faith are imbricated in politics.

3 Lecture notes. Compare his recent work, *Religion and the Constitution.*

So, then, a strong public presence and witness for religion was discouraged; but private practice, and freedom of conscience, was just fine. How did this regime play itself out over the years, through many twists, turns, permutations and contestations? There is no time for detail and, in any case, I am not a constitutional lawyer. So I will paint in rather broad strokes here. The main issue the Right Honourable Chief Justice has invited us to take up is often refracted in my country as "separation of church and state." For about a forty-year period, a group called "strong separationists" held sway, sometimes in public argumentation and, often enough, in constitutional adjudication. The strong separationist, then and now, seeks and favours not only a properly secular state (i.e., one in which no religion is established) but a thoroughly secularized society stripped of the public symbols, voices, and institutional presence of religion. There is today, however, a turning away from strong separationism in American constitutional adjudication. And it never did prevail in the realm of American political culture, for Americans realize that the logic of church-state separation on the constitutional level not only flounders but threatens to do real, even grievous, harm when applied to religion and politics more generally.

In his last major address before his death in 1996, Joseph Cardinal Bernardin of Chicago spoke at Georgetown University of the role of religion in American society. He pointed out the incoherence of claiming to respect religious belief while insisting that people keep it to themselves – precisely what a devout person cannot be expected to do. For religious faith is not a private matter: it is constitutive of a form of public membership in a church, temple, synagogue, or mosque. Persons of faith cannot bracket their beliefs when they enter the public square and should not be expected to do so. Cardinal Bernardin insisted that the logic of church-state separation not be extended to encompass religion and politics in the realm of civil society. Civil society involves the many networks, institutions, associations, and relationships that lie, to a great extent, beyond the purview of the state's writ in a pluralistic, constitutional order. As I have already indicated, it is a terrible mistake to carry over the logic of church-state separation into this realm. Were such separation to be fully effected, argued Cardinal Bernardin, we would be much poorer as a culture and a society. He went on to submit three ways in which religion plays a vital public role: in contributing to civil society through religiously based institutions in education, health care, and family services; in direct outreach to the poorest members of society; and, finally, in the realm of civic and moral formation as religion teaches service to one's neighbours and a sense of civic stewardship.[4]

In light of all this, I believe that "the dialectic of normative commitments," as the Right Honourable Chief Justice eloquently puts it, is (or should be) primarily a dialectic of *citizens*, variously located, through a culture of democratic argument: citizens engaging one another and sorting things out, as often they will, in a rather untidy, rough and ready way. The resort to the courts should be just that – a last resort – not the first move made in this dialectic. For it is likely to be true that an issue of religious and political importance that could be worked out informally becomes far more intractable if one group or another brings a test case seeking a controlling precedent. In such a circumstance the battle lines harden; the

---

4 Editor's note: An instructive comparison is afforded by the remarks of McLachlin C.J., writing for the majority in *Chamberlain v. Surrey School District No. 36*, [2002] 4 S.C.R. 710, at par. 19: "The Act's insistence on strict secularism does not mean that religious concerns have no place in the deliberations and decisions of the Board. Board members are entitled, and indeed required, to bring the views of the parents and communities they represent to the deliberation process. Because religion plays an important role in the life of many communities, these views will often be motivated by religious concerns. Religion is an integral aspect of people's lives, and cannot be left at the boardroom door. What secularism does rule out, however, is any attempt to use the religious views of one part of the community to exclude from consideration the values of other members of the community."

dialectic is frozen before it even begins to unfold. It is also worth noting here that, most often, from the religious side it is not adherence to a system claiming totality that is at stake in these matters; rather, what is at stake is an attempt to promote or defend a religiously derived sense of social justice as part of a normative vision for civil society, not as part of a particular creed that the believer wants to impose on everyone else. This makes it all the more important that civil authorities not circumscribe the boundaries of that dialectic in severe and a priori ways.

So: I want to suggest that the courts not "manage the dialectic" at all in a kind of preemptive strike but (where necessary) in a manner marked by considerable restraint. For the goods at stake are not best understood as totalistic religious goods versus totalistic legal and political goods but, rather, as competing understandings of a *public* good, variously derived. The rare case is one where religious conscience and society's values as manifested in the rule of law comprise opposite ends of a spectrum. The far more common case is putting together belief and law and bringing them to bear on one another. The best way to work this out is on the level of public deliberation and contestation rather than on the level of preemptive adjudication. Let a thousand arguments, dialogues, and debates bloom! The legal cases should be many fewer.

3

Religion and the Limits of Liberal Democracy

WILLIAM GALSTON

Consider the familiar phrase "liberal democracy."[1] The noun denotes a particular way of exercising public power; the adjective, a set of limitations on the exercise of that power. More broadly, the phrase directs our attention to two distinct dimensions of legitimate power: structure and scope. From this standpoint, government acts wrongly when it exceeds the scope of its rightful authority, even if the decision by which it does so is made in accordance with procedures that pass the test of structural legitimacy.

There are several possible ways of understanding the limits on the scope of authority. The most familiar is to point to, or posit, a list of core rights and liberties that the state is obligated to respect. A less familiar but perhaps ultimately more fruitful strategy is to begin by reflecting on the nature and diverse sources of legitimate authority, and then work our way towards a conception of zones that ought to be shielded from coercive intervention. I propose to move down this less trodden path, taking as the focus of my analysis the relation between liberal democratic government and civil associations, with particular attention to religious congregations and communities.

---

1 An earlier version of this paper was delivered as a Beatty lecture at McGill University, 9 October 2002.

LIBERAL DEMOCRACY AND CIVIL ASSOCIATION

A liberal democracy is, among other things, an invitation to struggle over the control of civil associations. State/society debates have recurred over the past century of US history, frequently generating landmark Supreme Court cases. While the specific issues vary, the general form is the same. On one side are general public principles that the state seeks to enforce; on the other are specific beliefs and practices that the association seeks to protect. *Boy Scouts of America v. Dale*[2] is the latest chapter in what will no doubt be a continuing saga.

Within the US constitutional context, these issues are often debated in terms such as free exercise of religion, freedom of association, or the individual liberty broadly protected under the Fourteenth Amendment. Rich and illuminating as it is, this constitutional discourse does not go deep enough. It is necessary to reconsider the understanding of politics that pervades much contemporary discussion, especially among political theorists – an understanding that tacitly views public institutions as plenipotentiary and civil society as a political construction possessing only those liberties that the polity chooses to grant and modify or revoke at will. This understanding of politics makes it all but impossible to give serious weight to the "liberal" dimension of liberal democracy.

The most useful point of departure for the reconsideration of politics I am urging is found in the writings of the British political pluralists and pluralist thinkers working in the Calvinist tradition.[3] This pluralist movement began to take shape in the nineteenth century as a reaction to the growing tendency to see state institutions as plenipotentiary. That tendency took various practical forms in different countries: French anti-

---

2 530 US 640 (2000).

3 For the British tradition, see Hirst, *Pluralist Theory of the State*. For the Calvinist tradition, see Skillen and McCarthy, *Political Order and the Plural Structure of Society*.

clerical republicanism; British parliamentary supremacy; the drive for national unification in Germany and Italy against subordinate political and social powers. Following Stephen Macedo (though disagreeing with him in other respects) I shall call this idea of the plenipotentiary state "civic totalism."[4]

Historically, one can discern at least three distinct secular theoretical arguments for civic totalism. (Theological arguments, which raise a further set of issues, are beyond the scope of these comments.) The first is the idea, traced back to Aristotle, that politics enjoys general authority over subordinate activities and institutions because it aims at the highest and most comprehensive good for human beings. The *Politics* virtually begins with the proposition that "all partnerships aim at some good, and ... the partnership that is most authoritative of all and embraces all the others does so particularly, and aims at the most authoritative good of all. That is what is called ... the political partnership." Whether this statement is an adequate representation of Aristotle's full view is a matter we may, for present purposes, set aside.

Hobbes offered a second kind of justification for civic totalism; namely, that any less robust form of politics would in practice countenance divided sovereignty – the dreaded imperium in imperio, an open invitation to civic conflict and war. Sovereignty cannot be divided, even between civil and spiritual authorities.[5] In Hobbes's view, undivided sovereign authority has unlimited power to decide whether, and under what conditions, individuals and associations would enjoy liberty of action. No entity, individual or collective, can assert rights against the public authority. Indeed, civil law may rightfully

---

4 For the full account of our agreement and (mainly) disagreement, see my review of Stephen Macedo's *Diversity and Distrust*, published in *Ethics* 112, 2 (January 2002): 386–91; and also Macedo's review of my *Liberal Pluralism*, published in *The American Prospect* ("The Perils of Diversity," 30 December 2002, 36–9).

5 *Leviathan*, "Of Commonwealth," chap. 29.

prohibit even the teaching of truth, if it is contrary to the requirements of civil peace.[6]

A third argument for civic totalism was inspired by Rousseau. Civic health and morality cannot be achieved without citizens' wholehearted devotion to the common good. Loyalties divided between the republic and other ties, whether to civil associations or to revealed religious truth, are bound to dilute civic spirit. And the liberal appeal to private life as against public life will only legitimate selfishness at the expense of the spirit of contribution and sacrifice without which the polity cannot endure. Representing this tradition, Émile Combes, a turn-of-the-century premier in the French Third Republic, declared: "There are, there can be no rights except the right of the State, and there [is], and there can be no other authority than the authority of the Republic."[7]

I do not wish to suggest that these three traditions converge on precisely the same account of civic totalism. A chasm divides Hobbes and Rousseau from Aristotle. To oversimplify drastically: Greek religion was civil, offering support for the institutions of the polis. The post-classical rise of revealed religion, especially Christianity, ruptured the unity of the political order. Much renaissance and early modern theory sought to overcome this diremption and restore the unity of public authority. Hobbes and Rousseau wrote in this "theological-political" tradition and tried in different ways to subordinate religious claims to the sovereignty of politics. For this reason, among others, Hobbes and Rousseau were less willing than was Aristotle to acknowledge the independent and legitimate existence of intermediate associations. They were drawn instead to a doctrine, originating in Roman law and transmitted to modernity through Bodin among others, according to which intermediate associations existed solely as revocable "concessions" of power from the sovereign political authority.

---

6 *Leviathan*, "Of the Kingdom of Darkness," chap. 46; compare "Of Commonwealth," chap. 17.

7 Quoted by J.N. Figgis in Hirst, *Pluralist Theory of the State*, 112.

Individuals possessed no inherent right of association, and associations enjoyed no rights other than those politically defined and granted. In short, intermediate associations were political constructions, to be tolerated only to the extent that they served the interests of the state. This Roman-law stance may be contrasted to the view of early Calvinists that a civil association required no special fiat from the state for its exist- ence. As Frederick Carney puts it: "Its own purposes, both natural and volitional, constitute its raison d'être, not its convenience to the state."[8]

These three traditions may seem far removed from the mainstream of contemporary views. Does not the liberal strand of "liberal democracy" qualify and limit the legitimate power of the state? Isn't this the entering wedge for a set of fundamental freedoms that can stand against the claims of state power?

The standard history of liberalism lends support to this view. The rise of revealed religion created a diremption of authority and challenged the comprehensive primacy of politics. The early modern wars of religion sparked new understandings of the relation between religion and politics, between individual conscience and public order, between unity and diversity. As politics came to be understood as limited rather than total, the possibility emerged that the principles constituting indi- vidual lives and civil associations might not be congruent with the principles constituting public institutions. The point of liberal constitutionalism, and of liberal statesmanship, was not to abolish these differences but, rather, so far as possible, to help them serve the cause of ordered liberty.

Despite this history, many contemporary theorists, including some who think of themselves as working within the liberal tradition, embrace propositions that draw them away from the idea of limited government and towards civic totalism, per- haps against their intention. Some come close to arguing that,

---

8 Carney, "Associational Thought in Early Calvinism," in Robertson, *Voluntary Associations*, 46.

if state power is exercised properly – that is, democratically –
then it need not be limited by any considerations other than
those required by democratic processes. Jürgen Habermas
offers the clearest example of this tendency. He insists that,
once obsolete metaphysical doctrines are set aside, "there is
no longer any fixed point outside the democratic procedure
itself." But this is no cause for worry or regret; whatever is
normatively defensible in liberal rights is contained in the
discourse-rights of "sovereign [democratic] citizens." The residual rights not so contained constitute not bulwarks against
oppression but, rather, the illegitimate insulation of "private"
practices from public scrutiny.[9]

THE PLURALIST ALTERNATIVE

It is in the context of questions such as these that political
pluralism emerges as an alternative to all forms of civic totalism. Political pluralism, to begin with, rejects efforts to understand individuals, families, and associations simply as parts
within and of a political whole. Likewise, it rejects the instru-
mental/teleological argument that individuals, families, and
associations are adequately understood as "for the sake of"
some political purpose. For example, religion is not civil
(only) and, in some circumstances, may be in tension with
civil requirements. This is *not* to say that political communities
must be understood as without common purposes. The political order is not simply a framework within which individuals,
families, and associations may pursue their own purposes. But
civic purposes are not comprehensive and do not necessarily
trump the purposes of individuals and groups.

Political pluralism understands human life as consisting in
a multiplicity of spheres, some overlapping, with distinct
natures and/or inner norms. Each sphere enjoys a limited but
real autonomy. It rejects any account of political community
that creates a unidimensional hierarchical ordering among

---

9 Quoted and discussed in Rawls, *Political Liberalism*, 379.

these spheres of life; rather, different forms of association and activity are complexly interrelated. There may be local or partial hierarchies among subsets of spheres in specific context, but there are no comprehensive lexical orderings among categories of human life.

For these reasons, among others, political pluralism does not seek to overcome but, rather, endorses the post-pagan diremption of human loyalty and political authority created by the rise of revealed religion. That this creates problems of practical governance cannot be denied. But pluralists refuse to resolve these problems by allowing public authorities to determine the substance and scope of allowable belief (Hobbes) or by reducing faith to civil religion and elevating devotion to the common civic good as the highest human value (Rousseau). Fundamental tensions rooted in the deep structure of human existence cannot be abolished in a stroke but must rather be acknowledged, negotiated, and adjudicated with due regard to the contours of specific cases and controversies.

Pluralist politics is a politics of recognition rather than of construction. It respects the diverse spheres of human activity; it does not understand itself as creating or constituting those activities. Families are shaped by public law, but that does not mean that they are "socially constructed." There are complex relations of mutual impact between public law and faith communities, but it is preposterous to claim that the public sphere creates these communities. Do environmental laws create air and water? Many types of human association possess an existence that is not derived from the state. Accordingly, pluralist politics does not presume that the inner structure and principles of every sphere must (for either instrumental or moral reasons) mirror the structure and principles of basic political institutions.

A pluralist politics is, however, responsible for coordinating other spheres of activity, and especially for adjudicating the inevitable overlaps and disputes among them. This form of politics evidently requires the mutual limitation of some freedoms, individual and associational. It monopolizes the legitimate use of force, except in cases of self-defence when the polity cannot or does not protect us. It understands that group tyranny is possible and therefore protects the individual against some associational abuses. But pluralist politics presumes that the enforcement of basic rights of citizenship and of exit rights (suitably understood) will usually suffice. Associational integrity requires a broad though not unlimited right of groups to define their own membership, to exclude as well as include, and a pluralist polity will respect that right.

A pluralist polity is not a neutral framework – assuming such a thing is even possible – but, rather, pursues a distinctive ensemble of public purposes. As David Nicholls, a leading scholar of political pluralism, argues, it presupposes a limited body of shared belief: in civil peace, in toleration for different ways of life, in some machinery for resolving disputes, and (notably) in the ongoing right of individuals and groups to resist conscientiously any exercise of public power they regard as illegitimate.[10] So understood, political pluralism serves as a barrier against the greatest preventable evils of human life, but it pursues at most a partial rather than a comprehensive good. That is my answer to one of the organizing questions of this collection of essays: the common good of a pluralist society is not merely the aggregate of individual and group interests, but it is not and must not be a *comprehensive* good either.

THE CONSTITUTIONAL POLITICS OF LIBERAL PLURALISM

The constitutional politics of liberal pluralism will restrict enforceable general norms to the essentials. By this standard, the grounds for national political norms and state intervention include: social order and physical security, the basic goods typically identified as necessary for any tolerable individual or collective life, and the components of shared national citizenship. It is difficult, after all, to see how societies can endure without some measure of order and material

---

10 Nicholls, *Pluralist State*, 123.

decency. And it has been agreed since Aristotle's classic discussion of the matter that political communities are organized around conceptions of citizenship that they must defend and that they must nurture through educational institutions as well as less deliberate and centralized formative processes.

But how much further should the state go in enforcing specific conceptions of justice, authority, or the good life? What kinds of differences should the state permit or perhaps even encourage and support? I suggest that an understanding of liberal democracy guided by the principle of political pluralism yields clear and challenging answers in specific cases.

Let me take a simple example. While many regret the exclusion of women from the Roman Catholic priesthood and from the rabbinate of Orthodox Judaism, political pluralism suggests that otherwise binding anti-discrimination laws should not be invoked to end these practices. What blocks the extension of these laws is the principle that religious associations enjoy considerable authority within their own sphere to order their own affairs and, in so doing, to express their understanding of spiritual reality. We can accept this principle of divided authority without necessarily endorsing the interpretations of gender roles and relations embedded in broader religious commitments.

This does not mean that all religiously motivated practices are equally deserving of accommodation or protection. Some clearly are not. Religious associations cannot be permitted to engage in human sacrifice; there can be no "free exercise" for Aztecs in a liberal society. Nor can such associations endanger the basic interests of children by withholding medical treatment in life-threatening situations. But there is a distinction between basic human goods, which the state must defend, and diverse conceptions of flourishing above that base-line, which the state should accommodate to the maximum extent possible. There is room for reasonable disagreement as to where that line should be drawn. But an account of liberal democracy built on a foundation of political pluralism should make us very cautious about expanding the scope of state power in ways that mandate uniformity.

THE PHILOSOPHICAL STATUS OF
POLITICAL PLURALISM

I would like to conclude with a question inspired by the late John Rawls. Is political pluralism along the lines I have just sketched a "comprehensive" account of these matters or, rather, a "political" account that can be assessed independently of controversial moral or metaphysical doctrines? I believe that Nicholls is on the right track when he argues that political pluralism is not fully a free-standing doctrine: "political pluralism may well be compatible with many ethical theories, but it is surely the case that it is incompatible with some ethical theories."[11] He goes on to observe, plausibly enough, that it "is likely that a monist in [moral or metaphysical] philosophy would reject political pluralism and would hope that the unity which is characteristic of the whole universe might become concrete in institutional form."[12]

Let me put this affirmatively. Political pluralism and value pluralism fit together in theory and in practice. Taken together, they offer the firmest basis for an account of liberal democracy that does justice to its "liberal" dimension, to its understanding of legitimate public power as important but inherently limited, and to the specific judgments (legal, legislative, and socio-cultural) that those thinking and acting in a liberal spirit are wont to reach.

---

11 Ibid., 105.
12 Ibid., 113.

4

Human Dignity and the Social Contract

DAVID NOVAK

THE DEMOCRATIC CONTRACT

To locate the original justification of a society in an agreement between its equal members has long been known as the idea of "the social contract." It is a highly attractive idea, as evidenced by the amount of discussion it has evoked for at least the past 400 years, especially during the past thirty years or so, ever since the publication of the most widely discussed work of political philosophy since John Stuart Mill's *On Liberty*; namely, John Rawls's *A Theory of Justice*, first published in 1971. Many contemporary political thinkers in democratic societies, who are loyal to their societies in principle, believe that this idea best explains how a democracy – especially *their* democratic polity – can cogently respect and defend the human rights of each one of its citizens. These rights are claims persons are justified in making on their societies before the latter can make any subsequent claims on them. As such, posterior social claims cannot contradict or sublate these prior personal claims without themselves becoming incoherent.

Respect and defence of human rights is considered to be the hallmark of a modern democracy. Respect and defence of these rights are what differentiates a modern constitutional democracy from democracy per se, which could be nothing more than the dictatorship of the majority, whether that dictatorship be spontaneously exercised by a mob (*demos*) or systematically exercised by a leader or leadership acting in the name of a mob. Such majority dictatorship is always conducted at the expense of the minorities who have no rights against it, no prior claims to make upon it.[1]

A democracy conceived to be based on a social contract presupposes that its parties come to it with rights which are *already* theirs. The contract itself is specifically designed to respect, defend, and even enhance these prior rights. Any attempt to rescind these rights puts the society in violation of its founding mandate, even if only a small minority might actually object to such rescission. Conversely, in any other society that is not based on the idea of a social contract, even where human rights are acknowledged, they are at best entitlements *from* the society rather than rights *before* the society. In such societies, human rights are a matter of social largesse or tolerance rather than something that the society must ever respect and defend. Therefore these rights can be rescinded by the society at will without it contradicting its founding mandate. Such a society can just as easily decide that these rights are useless as that they are useful. For this reason, it is simply insufficient to argue that "the assumption of natural rights [the older term for 'human rights' and a concession to the Lockean basis of Rawls's theory] is not a metaphysically ambitious one," that it is no more than a "hypothesis," and that it is only a "programatic decision," as we have been assured by Rawls's most prominent jurisprudential advocate, Professor Ronald Dworkin.[2]

Because the social contract stems from the rights of persons even prior to their becoming citizens of a democracy, a society based on a social contract can also respect and defend the

---

1 Compare Dworkin, *Taking Rights Seriously*, 205: "The institution of rights is therefore crucial, because it represents the majority's promise to the minorities that their dignity and equality will be respected ... [R]ights are ... the one feature that distinguishes law from ordered brutality."

2 "The Original Position," in Daniels, *Reading Rawls*, 46.

human rights of all human beings everywhere or anywhere. By virtue of simply being human, those other persons who are not now democratic citizens could in principle later become citizens of this or any democracy. Rights-based democracy, then, rests on an idea of human nature and is thus potentially global. The social contract presupposes that humans are by nature rational beings capable of making contracts and keeping them. That view of human nature has huge political consequences everywhere. The question arises, of course, whether human nature should be seen as something more than the mere capacity to make and keep contracts between humans themselves.

This emphasis on human rights is what makes modern constitutional democracy so very attractive in theory, especially to those minorities who have greatly benefitted from it in practice. Indeed, very few people today would want to live in anything but such a democracy. The other modern political alternatives (namely, fascism, communism, or clerical oligarchy) have proven to be disastrous for any society that has adopted them, and especially disastrous for any minorities who have found themselves having to live in such societies. As a Jew I can readily attest to this. For this reason alone, such minorities need to think out a democratic theory, especially a democratic social contract theory, as this seems to be the best basis for a rights-based democratic order. Only in that way can they be participants in a contractually based democratic social order in good faith and not just regard the benefits that have accrued to them as some sort of historical accident. But that must first be done in their own traditional terms and only thereafter in terms that can appeal to the rational persons who are taken to be actual or potential citizens of a democracy.

Unfortunately, though, most modern arguments for democracy, based as they have been on foundationally secularist premises, have not been formulated with much perspicacity, either theological or philosophical. Theologically, they have not shown how any tradition can authorize its members to participate in a social contract. And, as the British-American philosopher Alasdair MacIntyre has powerfully argued, we all come from traditions, whether we know it or admit it or not.[3] Philosophically, these modern arguments for democracy have been dependent on views of human nature that do not give a reason why any rational person should enter into a relationship of trust, like a contract, with any other rational person, even though these arguments have frequently recognized the social benefits of relations of trust. In other words, their admiration for trust has been more phenomenological than ethical; that is, they only describe *how* trust benefits society rather than *why* one ought to trust or be trusted.[4] In fact, most of these modern arguments for democracy have called for mistrust through their claims, both implicit and explicit, that members of traditional cultures need to break faith – that is, mistrust – their cultural origins in order to overcome them in civil society.

Thus most of these modern arguments for democracy have been recipes for the public disappearance of traditional communities. But without a traditional culture that is defensible not only theologically and philosophically but also publicly, individual members of these cultures do not have enough cultural capital to maintain their traditional identity even in private. For them, a democratic commitment turns out to be the sale of their very souls. That is why they need to argue for a traditional justification of a secular democratic order and, accordingly, avoid the type of apologetics that looks to that secular democratic order for their tradition's public justification. In other words, they need to argue for a finite secularity without embracing a secularist ideology.

What, then, is the current political value of the idea of a social contract? It would seem that the value of the idea of a social contract is that it is better able to justify a multicultural society than is any other idea of political authority. That is because the plurality built into the idea of multiculturalism is also built into the idea of the social contract. In the idea of

---

3 See MacIntyre, *Whose Justice? Which Rationality?* 334ff.
4 See, for example, Misztal, *Trust in Modern Societies,* 9ff.

the social contract as I am presenting it here the parties to it are not required to become parts of the whole that the contract itself creates; rather, they are participants in a multiplicity that they themselves create out of earlier commitments. These earlier social commitments are not overcome, nor are they meant to be overcome, in the social contract.[5]

Persons enter into a social contract not only *because* of these commitments but also (and equally) for the *sake* of them. If what people bring to the social contract are their pre-political cultural rights, which are their rights to be rooted in their original communities, then the social contract can be seen as an ongoing agreement as to what is necessary for different cultures to interact justly and peaceably with one another in a common political space but without having to give up their distinct identities to some sort of "melting pot." Indeed, it is from their experience in these original societies that such people derive their morality – not only the way they are to interact justly with other members of their community but also the way they are to interact justly with all others. Which is to say, their original societies prepare them for making such external agreements in the first place. This communitarian idea of the social contract should be more attractive to those who want civil society to respect their communality and not merely to foster their assimilation, individually or even collectively.

Conversely, the idea that civil society can and should construct its own culture will be seen as erroneous, both historically and philosophically.[6] Civil society depends rather on the plurality of cultures that in fact precede and transcend its construction through the social contract. The generation of secular space is the result of an intercultural agreement to

---

5 Conversely, Hobbes, Spinoza, Rousseau and Hegel assert, mutatis mutandis, that all original rights with which one entered civil society are turned over to the state. See Hobbes, *Leviathan*, chap. 21; Spinoza, *Tractatus Theologico-Politicus*, chap. 16; Rousseau, *The Social Contract*, 1.6; Hegel, *Philosophy of Right*, sec. 270.

6 Compare, however, Rorty, *Truth and Progress*, 195ff.

create a realm distinct from the sacred space of any primal community, one in which many cultures can take part but clearly without the creation of some new secular culture to replace the older cultures of the contracting parties. The very secularity of this new space – as distinct from the older spaces of traditional cultures – requires that it be participated in, as well as limited by, the members of the cultures who need such space for their own communal survival and flourishing. Thus a social contract is both necessary and desirable for the members of any historical culture still extant in the modern secular world, particularly in its nation-states. By means of such a social contract a historical culture can claim from civil society its prior right to continue to function as a primal community in the world. In return, it allows civil society to claim its loyalty and support through its political, economic, intellectual, and artistic efforts on behalf of all that society's citizens. That fits in quite well with the notion that a contract always involves mutual giving and taking. Furthermore, an intercultural social contract makes the political life of civil society far more exalted – and more inspiring – than does a social contract conceived in fundamentally economic terms. A society dedicated to the protection and enhancements of its participating cultures surely commands more respect and devotion than does a society established merely to protect and enhance property.

When, however, a civil society no longer respects that communal priority, it inevitably attempts to replace that sacred realm by becoming a sacred realm itself. As such, it attempts to become the highest realm in the lives of its citizens. In becoming what some have called a "civil religion," civil society usurps the role of historic traditions of faith. It becomes what it was never intended to be, for the hallmark of a democratic social order is the continuing limitation of its governing range.[7] Without such limitation, any society tends to expand its government

---

7 For the first use of the term "civil religion" (but not the concept), see Rousseau, *The Social Contract*, 4.8; also, Spinoza, *Tractatus Politicus*, 3.10.

indefinitely. But such limitation cannot come from within; it can only come from what is both outside it and above it.[8] Today that external and transcendent limitation can be found in the freedom of citizens in a democracy to find their primal identity by being and remaining a part of their traditional communities. This is what has come to be known in democracies as religious liberty. Membership in these traditional communities is outside the range of civil society because they have historical precedence, and it is above the range of civil society because of the ontological status given these communities through their relationship with God. Indeed, these communities claim both ancient and cosmic privileges. This is what both limits the secular and, within its limited range, entitles it.

A CONTRACT BETWEEN MINORITIES

Multiculturalism, as I would like to understand it, assumes that all the bearers of the various cultures participating in the social contract are minorities. Any notion of a majority rule, except for purposes of election to public office, legislation, or judicial decision, requires the type of monoculture that is inimical to the cultural rights of any and all minorities. Surely multiculturalism is for the sake of minority groups.[9] Only when that logic is carried further does it also function for the sake of the individual person and his or her rights. The individual person is the smallest minority possible but not the only minority possible. As such, the individual only functions as a rights-bearer in cases involving certain limited political, legal, or economic claims. But in cases involving larger social claims, such as religious liberty or domestic sanctity, cultural rights – which are the claims of persons to be able to exercise their

---

8 For the idea that all limitation is external, see Ludwig Wittgenstein, *Tractatus Logico-Philosphicus*, 5.61. Compare Immanuel Kant, *Critique of Pure Reason*, B295.

9 See D. Novak, "The Jewish Ethical Tradition and the Modern University," *Journal of Education* 180, 3 (1998): 22–38.

cultural identity both in their primal communities and in the
secular realm – much more is at issue.[10] And, more often than
not, the minorities by themselves and between themselves can
reach a consensus without the literal designation of a majority
conclusion. Certainly that is the case with a social contract as
distinct from a formal political pact. The social contract is not
adjudicated in a court or argued in a legislature, even though
its informal negotiations in the larger civil society often have
judicial and legislative effects.

No contract between persons – be it a private contract
between individual parties or a public contract between all
parties to the society – can claim to be the most original or
enduring social bond. Indeed, without the presupposition of
prior and more basic social bonds, the idea of the social contract becomes incoherent. This is because only persons can
contract with one another. Persons are social beings by nature
not by mutual agreement,[11] and there cannot be contracting
human persons who are not *already* socialized. Hence no contract between persons can create an original society because
an original society must already exist before there are contractual relations between the persons within it, much less
between persons crossing over the borders and coming
together from different original societies. However, this pre-
contractual social reality does not preclude a subsequent social
contract. In fact, it can encourage the formulation of subsequent social contracts. One can derive a very positive evaluation indeed of the democratic social contract from the sources
of traditional religious cultures like Judaism and Christianity,
and from simultaneous reasoning about general human social

---

10 See Taylor, *Multiculturalism*, 61.
11 The phrase "social beings by nature" is borrowed from Aristotle
(*Politics* 1.1/1251b1ff.), but my use of it differs from his in that,
for me, familial-communal life transcends civil society (for Aristotle,
the polis) rather than being subordinate to it (cf. *Nicomachean
Ethics* 8.9/1162a15–20) – or, ideally, being obliterated by it (cf.
Plato, *Republic* 485Eff.).

experience (when conducted with theological and philosophical perspicacity). This requires the presentation of the most cogent justification of the idea of a social contract, one whose very cogency claims neither too much nor too little.

COMMUNITY AND SOCIETY

The difference between an original and a contractual human association is the difference between a community, or *Gemeinschaft*, and a society, or *Gesellschaft*. This is something that modern sociologists have often discussed since the terms were conceptualized by the German social theorist Ferdinand Tönnies.[12] The difference between these terms can be most clearly located in the difference between how a merely contractual society deals with familial identity and how an original society deals with it.

Under ordinary circumstances our original society, our primal community, *is* our natural family. That is why our greatest childhood fear is orphanhood or even less radical familial break-ups (e.g., divorce): they entail the loss of our community in its most original manifestation. That is also why a community (*Gemeinschaft*) is looked upon as an extended family more than as a negotiated amalgamation of separate families.[13] To be sure, one can see this original condition as something to be developed or as something to be overcome; it can be affirmed or denied in a variety of ways. But much social contract theory, whether explicitly or implicitly, has avoided considering the family as the most immediate and persistent locus of one's primal community.[14] It has continued to regard

---

12 See Tönnies, *Community and Society*.

13 Compare Aristotle, *Politics*, 1.1/1252b15–35.

14 Accordingly, it cannot recognize the fact that even those who believe they have overcome their communal origins most often find another community in which to be reborn. Frequently that is done through marriage, remarriage, or religious conversion, which are the most basic ways of altering one's communal status.

the parties to the social contract as lone individuals who are only the bearers of rights.

The familial status of these lone individuals is a matter of privacy; indeed, the right to privacy becomes the greatest of all rights. But since "privacy" is that which is abstracted (*privatio*) from the public realm (*res publica*), public considerations ultimately trump the interests of the family, so conceived, on every front, just as they trump privacy itself. In fact, where familial structures have no acknowledged priority, there is a tendency among secularist democratic theorists to want to redefine the family altogether. And that despite the remarkable consensus among traditional cultures as to what the family is; namely, a procreative union for the sake of bearing and raising the children that that union hopes to bring into the world. Indeed, one finds this traditional consensus under heavy attack in current democratic discourse.[15] The question is whether civil society can radically redefine the family as its own institution, though the family is an institution civil society receives from historical cultures. Certainly there are contractual elements involved in family structure, even in traditional societies. But to reduce familial existence to a series of contractual arrangements is to belittle it and to detract from the richness of an existence many people very much desire.[16]

If the family is no more than a unit of a contractual society, then why should it not be looked upon as one more private contract within a larger (public) contractual realm? Yet if that notion were made known to most members of democratic

---

15 See, for example, Andrew Koppelman, "Sexual and Religious Pluralism," in Olyan and Nussbaum, *Sexual Orientation and Human Rights in American Religious Discourse,* 215ff. (Editor's note: In this light, compare "Statement on the Status of Marriage in Canada," 18 June 2003 <www.marriageinstitute.ca>, of which Professor Novak is a signatory.)

16 Perhaps that desire explains why, in a recent survey of movie-goers, their all-time favourite film turned out to be Mario Puzo's *The Godfather.*

societies, whose families form the central locus of their primal communities (which are for them both necessary and desirable), they would surely find contemporary social contract theory to be morally repugnant. In other words, they would reject it by means of the most basic democratic phenomenon: majority approval or disapproval.[17] Very few people, for example, would really want their children to be wards, de facto if not yet de jure, of the institution of contractual society – the state. Yet that is the most obvious result of looking at the liberty of the family as something to be overcome in the institution of society. What must also be recognized is that familial liberty, as something prior to the founding of civil or contractual society, is intimately linked to religious liberty. Most people regard their familial bonds and their religious bonds alike as having a sanctity beyond the reach of civil society and its expression in the state. Indeed, most people regard their familial bonds to be part of their religious bonds.[18]

The only cultural minorities who can resist the inner tendency of the secular state to turn all alternative societies into private corporations within its own purview – *Gesellschaften* – are religious minorities. Indeed, it is the distinction between culture as religiously founded and culture as racially founded that enables a minority religiously defined culture to resist the totalizing expansion of civil society. Cultures that are racially

---

17 Even minority rights, which are prior to the founding of civil society, must still be accepted by the majority of the members of that society in order for them to be politically effective.

18 Surely that is not something they would cogently claim for their property, whose very function is defined by the currency the state issues and which is wholly taxable by the state. When it comes to marriage, on the other hand, most people want it to be a sacred covenant or a sacrament, which may help to explain why the growing number of North Americans who want something less than an existential commitment in their sexual relationships usually opt out of both religious and civil marriage, eschewing the blessings and demands of both church and state.

defined, by contrast, either claim some special privileges
within civil society, usually as the result of a claim for compen-
sation for past racial persecution, or they attempt to dominate
it by absorbing it into themselves. This is inevitably done
through the simultaneous exclusion and persecution – even
extermination – of those races whom they perceive to be inferior. Unlike religious cultures, who define themselves by their
founding, sustaining, and fulfilling relationship with God,
racial cultures inevitably define themselves in relation to their
persecutors or their victims.

I can think of no better expression of the political and cultural inadequacies of both economically based liberal ideologies and racist mythologies than the following magnificent
insight of the French philosopher Jacques Maritain. This was
composed in 1942, a time when one racist culture could have
destroyed our multicultural civilization and when liberal ideology proved to be inadequate to counter the evil such racism
presented:

In the bourgeois individualist type of society there is no ... form of
communion. Each one asks only that the State protect his individual
freedom of profit ... Nor in the racial type of community ... Nothing
is more dangerous than such a community: deprived of a determining
objective, political communion, [it] will carry its demands to the infinite, will absorb and regiment people, swallow up in itself the religious
energies of the human being. Because it is not defined by a work to
be done, it will only be able to define itself by its opposition to other
human groups. Therefore, it will have essential need for an enemy
against whom it will build itself; it is by recognizing and hating its
enemies that the political body will find its common consciousness.[19]

Even though religiously based cultures also have the tendency either to withdraw from or to dominate others, unlike
racially based cultures they have within themselves the
resources to live in good faith in a multicultural society, where

---

19 Maritain, *The Rights of Man and Natural Law,* 122f.

no one culture is civilly, politically, or legally privileged over any other culture. That is because religiously based cultures have an idea of universal human personhood as the "image of God" – understood as a relationship with God – that is not their own peculiar domain.[20] As such, adherents of each of these cultures can accept the fact that other cultures enable their members to function as the image of God, even though each of these adherents needs to believe that his or her own culture does that best. Indeed, it is only those religious cultures who do claim a totally exclusive relationship with God that tend to become racist-like in their attempts to withdraw from or dominate others (even in civil society).

One might very well see the beginnings of the multicultural pluralism required for civil society's social contract as located in inter-religious reverence. And that reverence can only be genuine, and not merely a rhetorical instrument, when it is the result of each community being able to apprehend a universal horizon out of its own traditional sources. On that horizon it discovers other cultures and their human integrity. Only a civil society that is largely made up of such religious people is in any position to respect the universal transcendence of such communal origins and such communal destinies. Thus, it seems to me, only religious people in a democratic society have sufficient reasons for ensuring the limitation of the normative reach of that society. Racially based cultures have no such cosmic orientation and cannot, therefore, command any such civil respect. Needless to say, cultures based on class or gender, having even less of a cosmic orientation than civil society itself, can claim even less respect because they are ideological constructs lacking either historical or ontological roots. Like races, they can only function as special interest groups within civil society, which are then subject to civil tolerance or intolerance according to what is currently perceived to be "politically correct." Usually, this trendy type of political conformism is the

---

20 See Novak, *Natural Law in Judaism*, 167–73.

province of an elitist subculture rather than the stance of the
civil society itself.

Whereas, when one begins with society, there is no real
place for community, when one begins with community there
is the potential to make a real place for society. In other words,
when one sees civil society to be the primary human association, it is impossible to recognize community as being anything more than a matter of privacy, which itself is a societal
entitlement. The moral priority of community, then, will be
vigorously denied. But of course no historical community
could possibly accept this construction of the matter in good
faith. A historical, religiously constituted community asks for
more than tolerance: it asks for respect. And when one sees
community to be the primary human association, one can
certainly respect the secondary importance of society, which is
what many civil societies have in fact asked for themselves. It
is expressed in the value that many democratic citizens see in
the idea of "limited government."

Furthermore, the primacy of civil society inevitably requires
the creation of a hypothetical – that is, a fictitious, even mythical – "state of nature," or "original [individual] position," as its
starting point.[21] The primacy of community, on the other hand,
which does lead to civil society, can be located in history, and
that historical origin has by no means been overcome. For any
theory, a real point of departure is preferable to a hypothetical
one. But secularist social contract theory cannot claim historical priority, let alone ontological priority. It is rooted neither in
history nor in nature but only in the human imagination.

Civil society as secular space can emerge out of intercultural
agreement because cultures or primal communities have a
need for that space. Communities are rarely, if ever, politically, economically, or intellectually self-sufficient. In one way
or another, they need to make alliances with others outside
their own cultural domain – alliances in which neither party

---

21 See Rawls, *Theory of Justice*, 13–22; compare Novak, *Natural Law
in Judaism*, 22f.

dominates the other and no party or combination of parties is forced to become an anonymous third entity. Communities need to engage in foreign relations if they do not want to be vulnerable to political, economic, or intellectual conquest or to stagnating isolation. This is done through continual negotiation. Negotiation, of course, is the stuff of any contract, including the social contract.

All of this requires the creation of neutral or secular space in order to conduct these negotiations and to implement their conclusions. However, what is lost on most social contract theorists is the fact that political, economic, and intellectual interests are all for the sake of cultural survival and development. Ultimately, any community's will to live depends on the desire of its members to preserve and advance their traditional way of life as an ontological desideratum, one that is grounded in an original divine revelation and that sees itself as being in the vanguard of universal redemption by God. Political, economic, and intellectual pursuits are for the sake of that end. Thus, from the standpoint of a religious culture, participation in a civil society (or a larger civilization of civil societies) is necessary but not sufficient for human flourishing. Participation in civil society can also be seen as a means to a greater end, which is quite consistent with the limited aims of a democratic society, which should never regard its programs, no matter how serious, as being of ultimate importance for the lives of its citizens. Democracy's goals cease to be democratic when they are made into anything more than penultimate temporal ends.

FREEDOM AND AUTONOMY

One of the main misconceptions about a traditional community (or people) is that participation in civil society is required in order to liberate persons from roles they have not freely accepted for themselves. The fact is, however, that even in the most traditional community one is still free to accept or reject such roles in a variety of ways. Participation in civil society builds upon that freedom of choice, to be sure, but it is not its

first occasion. In other words, participation in civil society is not
the origin of what might be seen as political freedom of choice.

The human environment, or community, in which we live
has been determined for us by others, yet it is also something
we are free to determine for ourselves. Initially our worldly
locale is determined for us since we could not have chosen
our birth or our birthplace for ourselves. Our communal origins, like our biological origins, are already there for us without any consent on our part. Nevertheless, whenever we do
become aware of our freedom to choose among multiple possibilities in the world, we eventually learn that the most important possibility is the option of whether or not we want to be
situated in our original society at all. It is a momentous discov-
ery that the initial social status given to us as children is not
necessarily the only one available to us as adults. At this point,
we have two fundamental possibilities: we can either identify
with our community or we can repudiate it. The choice is to
be there or not to be there. There is also the subsequent
choice of *how* we want to be there or not be there. The first
choice is generic; the subsequent choices are specific.

These choices are made for or against a moral authority
rather than a coercive authority. Coercive authority speaks by
threats of violence; hence one obeys it in order to avoid harm.
As such, it is essentially restraining rather than encouraging.
Moral authority, on the other hand, speaks persuasively; hence
one obeys it because one wants to respond favourably to someone to whom one is genuinely attracted. As such, this form of
authority is essentially positive, encouraging rather than
restraining. Even when moral authority issues negative com-
mandments ("thou shalt nots"), it does so for the sake of
higher positive ends. Only moral authority offers an option
that can be adopted out of love and not just out of fear of
consequences.[22] And no community can function well, or
even survive, unless a large number of its members love it and
the source of its moral authority. Of course, every community

---

22 See *Babylonian Talmud*: Shabbat 88a.

has to have its own forms of social coercion to deal with those members of the community who want the benefits of the community without abiding by its rules. Nevertheless, communal coercion only works when it is required for a small number of people and for a small amount of public time. When coercion is required more often than not, the community becomes a prison, inviting the repudiation of its authority by more and more of its members until it ceases to function as a community at all.

In biblical terms, this means that there is always some sort of covenant (*berit*) operating between the community and God, and simultaneously among the members of the community itself. Unlike a contract, this covenant is not initiated by the mutual agreement of equals; and unlike a contract, a covenant is interminable. The community is there before any of its members are born or reborn into it, and the community will survive the loss of any of its members. Nonetheless, such a covenant requires the free acceptance of communal authority in order for the covenant to work.[23] Free acceptance, rather than an egalitarian agreement, is the aspect of a covenant that enables the idea of a contract – especially a social contract – to emerge. Agreement between equals presupposes that one has been unequal beforehand and that, in some ways, remains unequal. Thus children only learn to appreciate the equal status of their siblings (and then their friends, and then strangers) when they have first appreciated that the unequal authority of parents made it possible. In other words, their equals have parents too. Furthermore, children must be able to trust the authority that is over them before they will be able to trust those who are their equals and will be their equals when they become adults. It is the possibility of mutual trust, freely given and freely accepted, that causes a contract to be initiated and sustained in a promise. It is only when this non-coercive, intelligent, and benevolent

---

23 See Novak, *The Election of Israel*, 163ff. For a further development of the argument of this chapter see my forthcoming book, *The Jewish Social Contract*.

heteronomy is acknowledged that we can speak of the type of political autonomy that a social contract recognizes. One can only accept a human-made normative order when it attempts to imitate a normative order that is not of human making, even though it substantiates human being.

5

Persons, Politics, and a Catholic Understanding of Human Rights

JEAN BETHKE ELSHTAIN

Human beings are soft-shelled creatures. All bodies are fragile. But some bodies in some circumstances are more vulnerable than others.

In Argentina, during its period of the so-called "dirty war" in the late seventies and early eighties, young people were the most vulnerable, the most likely to be "disappeared" – a horrible and dreaded word that then entered the political vocabulary as part of the gallery of horrors of human mistreatment of other humans. Young men were the most vulnerable of all. Over two-thirds of the "disappeared" were men.

Those who rose to protest these disappearances were women, Las Madres, the Mothers of the Plaza. Because of the potency of the symbol of "the mother" in Roman Catholic societies, women had not only symbolic authority but also at least partial insulation from the violence of the regime. How would it look to attack a group of mothers looking for their lost children? Mothers weren't exempt, of course, but mothers openly marching in a public place were more difficult to assault openly than would have been a group of men, of fathers. The language in which Las Madres protested these disappearances was double and universal in each instance: the language of a mother's grief and the language of human rights. We see in such circumstances both how necessary are human rights, and how weak a reed when tyrants are determined to harm and to harm egregiously. Nevertheless, we cannot do without the cry that takes shape when one's rights, one's very dignity as a person, are under assault.

Take a second example. In her powerful prison memoirs, *Eyes of the Tailless Animals*, so-called because prisoners in North Korea's extensive gulags and torture centres are called "tailless animals" and reduced to less than human status, Soon Ok Lee writes of a prison cell in which she found herself after she had survived a series of horrendous tortures:

Six pregnant women were lying on the cold cement floor, which was not even covered with a mat. I thought, even animals receive better treatment outside this prison. The women were giving birth to their babies. The babies were supposed to be stillborn. Because Kim Il Sung had ordered that all anti-Communists be eliminated within three generations, prison policy said that prisoners, who were considered anti-Communists by definition, could not have babies in prison. When pregnant women came to prison, they were forced to abort their babies. Poison was injected into the babies cuddled in their mothers' wombs. After the injection, the pregnant woman suffered tremendous pain until the babies were stillborn about twenty-four hours later. Medical officers walked around the pregnant women and kicked their swollen bellies if they screamed or moaned.

Miraculously, some of the babies were born alive. They cried like normal babies do. When a live baby was born, a medical officer said to the medical prisoners, "Kill it! These criminals don't have any right to have babies. What are you doing? Kill it right now!"

The mothers of these new-born babies just laid on the floor and sobbed so helplessly while a medical prisoner's shaking hands twisted the baby's neck. The babies struggled for a short second, but they died so easily. Male prisoners wrapped the babies in rags and dumped them into a basket.

I was shocked. This was the most cruel human behavior I had ever seen in my life. Even today, I dream about the women who had just given birth to their babies.[1]

---

1 Soon Ok Lee, *Eyes of the Tailless Animals*, 90f.

Soon Ok Lee is one of the few to survive the North Korean gulag. Most prisoners die within four months. She entered a bewildered if convinced communist, wondering why she had been singled out (evidently the local commissar simply had a quota to meet and trumped up some charges against her because he was irritated with her for refusing him a favour), and she escaped a committed Christian. She became a Christian while in prison because she saw how Christians were particularly singled out for abuse, yet how they loved one another, even in that hell on earth. And because, thinking of those babies who survived attempted coerced abortion, crying feebly, their necks being wrung – "they died so easily" – she yearned for a way to lift up human dignity.

Whether in the gulags of North Korea or the torture centres in Buenos Aires or in any of the other hells on earth, past and present, human dignity needs a guarantee. There are particular violations meted out to helpless prisoners, like those fragile new-borns and their sobbing mothers, that cause the language of rights, even a powerful account of rights, to seem so inadequate, so puny, so nearly irrelevant, because something so deep is being violated: something intrinsic to, and constitutive of, our very humanity. Pope John Paul ii has told us repeatedly over the course of his great human rights pontificate that, when we find ourselves face-to-face with another human being, we must "pause at the irreducible." Many do not pause. Many do far worse.

This irreducibility compels us, however, to go on speaking of human rights. But what kind of rights shall we speak about? What account of rights shall we try to give? If the concept of human rights is now indelibly engrained at all levels of public discourse, its gravamen differs widely. Let us ask ourselves first what version of rights yields what sort of rights culture. Then we may reflect on what culture of rights most deeply recognizes our intrinsic dignity, our profound sociality, and our equally profound vulnerability; and why, therefore, this rights culture is most open to the concerns I am trying to raise.

What construals of rights underlie, or are at least consistent with, what versions of a human rights culture? There can be a culture of which we may say (in good Rortian fashion) "things just happen to have worked out this way." Here rights talk begins to sound a bit like a shopping list. Rights keep on proliferating to the point that it becomes difficult to keep up with them as different groups of claimants push claims they choose to couch in the language of particular rights that apply specifically, perhaps even exclusively, to themselves: all of this by contrast to rights that speak to a broad category that applies to all human beings without exception.

Do we really require separate rights that appertain in light of what I learned in graduate school to call "ascriptive characteristics" – those things about us that are accidents of birth? Race and gender are two examples of the latter. To be human, by contrast, is no accident of birth; it is definitional of it. Humanness is the great leveller. Who belongs definitionally within the category "human"? Have we lost confidence in our humanness to do the necessary legal and political work?

We may leave these questions hanging in the air and turn to consider the power and robustness of a very different version of human rights that flows from Roman Catholic social teaching. The great encyclicals in which that teaching is found are addressed to "all persons of goodwill" and are said to apply to "all without definition." They are offered to Christians and non-Christians alike as a way to articulate and defend a culture that sustains human rights for all people.

Let us begin with an appeal to *Dignitatis Humanae* (1995). This Vatican II document opens by proclaiming the dignity of the human person and affirming that that dignity involves "enjoying and making use of responsible freedom, not driven by coercion but motivated by a sense of duty." Already we see a difference. Duty and the rightful exercise of rights are not severed from one another, as is so often the case in our regnant rights talk, from which any correlative notion of duty has been expunged. Contemporary rights talk correlates rights wants and preferences. It doing so it is indebted to a contractarianism that posits the self as primordially "free," where freedom is understood (in the classic works of Hobbes and

Rousseau, at least) as a condition of asociality.[2] Hobbes, and others associated with radical nominalism, saw persons as entities driven by irresistible desires and a "restless seeking of power after power that ceaseth only in death."[3] Any rights culture derived from such premises becomes a way we confront and are protected from one another. There is no mutual and objective "orientation toward freedom" in this view, whereas in Roman Catholic social teaching the context within which rights are located is undeniably teleological, in the sense that there is a good towards which we tend and, hence, an intrinsic connection between truth, reason, human rights, and freedom – an altogether different sort of culture.

To deepen the contrast between nominalist rights talk (if we may call it that) and the alternative promoted in Roman Catholic thought, we need to consider three things: (1) anthropological presuppositions, or views of the human person; (2) the "rights" concept itself; and (3) the good towards which rights tend. If my treatment of these things is in any way compelling, it will help to reveal a late modern dilemma. We cannot do without human rights. But the way in which rights are generally understood may not be capable of sustaining appreciation of human rights at the most fundamental level. This is because too much of the deep background and justification for them has been jettisoned along the way.[4]

---

2 Freedom, for Hobbes, means to be free from external impediment to one's progress. Rousseau has a version of freedom in which one's social entanglements (with women certainly) wind up corrupting one, sapping natural vigour and liberty.

3 Hobbes, *Leviathan*, "Of Man," chap. 11.

4 Much of this background and justification is of course religious or theological, which helps to explain why it has been jettisoned. In a pluralistic society, we want human equality and rights, as protected in statutory law, to stand on their own, so to speak. But Michael Perry, for one, goes so far as to contend that "there is no intelligible (much less persuasive) secular version of the conviction that every human being is sacred; the only intelligible versions are religious" (*The Idea of Human Rights*, 11).

ANTHROPOLOGICAL PRESUPPOSITIONS

When I was in graduate school it was still possible to talk about contrasting views of human nature without being accused of that most dire of all contemporary sins, essentialism. Perhaps we have thrown out way too much by clapping a strict censorship over words like "nature" and "the natural" in the erroneous assumption that all those who evoke nature or the natural are committed to the view that human beings are not shaped in any fundamental way by their social and political worlds and their historic time and place. This is balderdash. When we speak of anthropology, we talk about what sort of creature we are, and we can do this without smuggling in a strict determinism.

Clearly we need some definite view of human being and of human persons – to speak of their irreducibility does not relieve us of this requirement – in order to speak coherently of human rights. We might make our approach by acknowledging, as I did at the outset, our fragility; or by taking an Augustinian route and talking about how deeply we are "pressed" by the world. But we can do all of this even as we frame considerations of our humanity with a strong notion of the good towards which human being tends and of the plural goods that reflect a higher or highest good and draw us closer to it. To evoke anthropology in this teleological way is certainly to remain open to cultural and historical specificity and to the role of contingency in human affairs; to speak of the contingent and to speak of the natural are not mutually exclusive alternatives.[5] Ironically, it may also be the only way to remain open to the fact that coherent rights talk is lodged in a presupposition of human dignity that locates us in a world with others – that is, in a universe rather than in an ultimately isolating multiverse of mere individuals.

---

5   Thus, for example, we may wish to speak of the human being as intrinsically, not contingently, social; we are born to relationality. Yet we are indeed *born*, and our sociality and relationality is actualized in and with a set of historical contingencies.

This teleological approach makes sense of the linkage between rights and duties, and combines with other features of Roman Catholic anthropology to steer us towards a different understanding of freedom. As Lisa Cahill puts it, if the modern social encyclicals "affirm much more strongly the importance of the individual and ... of his or her rights" than do older documents, nevertheless these rights are not spoken of "primarily as individual claims against other individuals or [against] society. They are woven into a concept of community that envisions the person as a distinctive part of overlapping communities. Rights exist within a historic and social context and they are intelligible in terms of the obligations of persons to one another within that context."[6] On such a vision, commonality is assumed and solidarity is an achievement. What wants explaining is not solidarity but isolation. By contrast, those oriented to the views embedded in nominalist rights talk strain mightily to figure out how such essentially selfish creatures as human beings might actually relate to one another in relatively decent ways.

For all the lip service to social context in the contemporary rights culture, it is characterized by an undeniable individualist thrust.[7] That is because the self is sovereign and has a proprietary interest in itself. It is above all a choosing self, and its own choices are paramount. Speech, even human rights speech, thus becomes a monologue and not a dialogue.[8] But does this self-sovereignty really serve any person well? There is, to be sure, an insight in this account of human beings that is worth preserving; namely, that we really do become, in some profound sense, what we choose. But the problem with the emphasis on choice is that choice itself is impoverished by being reduced to the dictates of desire or preference without

6 Lisa Sowle Cahill, "Toward a Christian Theory of Human Rights," *Journal of Religious Ethics* 9 (Fall 1980): 284; compare p. 278. Such a perspective in part accounts for the preference within Roman Catholic social thought for the term "person" over the (liberal and libertarian) concept of the "individual."

7 Compare Glendon, *Rights Talk*.

8 The abortion debate, for example, displays all these characteristics.

any necessary reference to goods, ends, and purposes or to how one might distinguish the more from the less worthy: there is no normative ordering of goods. The "sovereign self" concept also casts a pall of suspicion over ties of reciprocal obligation and mutual interdependence, with which women especially have long been associated. Over time, I submit, it erodes friendship, families, civil society, polities, and even markets. This erosion of genuine community invites what William Galston calls "the plenipotentiary state" – a Leviathan that accrues ever more power to itself and knows not when, or where, or why to stop.

For its part, Roman Catholic thought moves in a different direction. Given its emphasis on the sociality of the self, and on the teleological dimensions of the human person, it speaks throughout of *responsible* freedom realized through multiple associations with their respective authoritative claims. It speaks, as John Paul II noted at a plenary assembly of the Sacred College of Cardinals in 1979, of a positive freedom that opens out into love:

Very often, freedom of will and the freedom of the person are understood as the *right to do anything*, as the right not to accept any norm or any duty that involves commitment... But Christ does not teach us such an interpretation and exercise of freedom. The freedom of each individual creates duties, demands full respect for the hierarchy of values, and is potentially directed to the Good without limits, to God. In Christ's eyes, freedom is not first of all "freedom from" but "freedom for." The full enjoyment of freedom is love, in particular the love through which individuals give themselves.

All of this has an impact, of course, on the way in which rights and the relation between rights is construed in Roman Catholic social teaching.

RIGHTS, UNDERSTOOD HOW?

Absent some account of the human good it is hard to know what rights are all about. Telling us what rights are all about

– the explicit recognition of our intrinsic dignity – provides a good bit of the heft and lift of the argument here being sketched. Does it make any great difference whether that dignity is rooted in the freedom we have from and for God or, say, in the autonomy of the human will? We have already touched on some of the consequences of deploying rights to institutionalize the autonomy of the will, and that is a matter to which we will return in a moment. For now it need only be said that perhaps the primary consequence is to place all declared rights on a par with each other. Not so in Roman Catholic teaching, which acknowledges a hierarchy of rights corresponding, in its way, to the hierarchy of goods. At the top of this hierarchy is the right to freedom of religion. *Dignitatis* (§2) declares that, for all persons, the right to religious freedom has priority because this right speaks most pointedly to the *Urgrund* of human rights; namely, the ordering of our very selves, in our created nature, to the truth, and "especially religious truth."

"The right to religious freedom," we are told, "has its foundation not in the subjective disposition of the person but in his very nature." John Paul II comments that *Dignitatis* expresses "not only the theological concept of the question but also the concept reached from the point of view of natural law, that is to say from the 'purely human' position, on the basis of premises given by human experience, human reason, and our sense of human dignity."[9] Yet this objectivist way of talking about rights and dignity is today unintelligible to many.[10] The right to religious freedom may be a well marked entry in the human rights lexicon, but its ordering and orienting power is far from evident. It is no longer understood, as it ought to be, how creating

---

9 See Filibeck, *Human Rights in the Teaching of the Church,* 161f.

10 Editor's note: compare the subjectivist approach that, under the Charter, has become operative in Canadian jurisprudence, as *per* Iacobucci J. (*Law v. Canada* [1999] 1 S.C.R. 497, par. 53): "the equality guarantee in s. 15(1) is concerned with the realization of personal autonomy and self-determination. Human dignity means that an individual or group feels self-respect and self-worth."

immunities from state control over religion makes possible a
form of human flourishing that is otherwise unattainable; how
other rights and freedoms depend for their health on this one.

In the American Constitution, the first prominent mention
of rights is the Bill of Rights, which revolves largely around
civic freedoms (of assembly, press, and speech) and concerns
primarily what government cannot do to you. It is surely no
accident, however, that the First Amendment concerns religion: free exercise plus non-establishment. This assumes communities of believers free from external control. It suggests –
does it not? – that the regime of rights cannot be sustained by
rights alone. It needs both selves and communities of certain
kinds. Yet rights talk in the United States today is highly indi-
vidualistic and almost infinitely plastic, which brings us back
to the question of consequences.

Absent a way to sift and winnow rights, rights easily become
distorted and even trivialized. The shopping cart approach, as
I said, puts all declared rights on a par. The "right" to a state-
funded vacation may take its place alongside the rights to religious and political freedom or the right to be free from torture. What is worse, in a world defined by rights as adversarial
possessions, human identity itself is flattened out. We are all
said to be nothing but bundles of needs and claims. On this
view, what separates us from one another is not our human
distinctiveness but the fact that some are cast as powerful,
others as powerless; some as hegemonic, others as victims.
Rights are what we use to "get ours." In the process we lose
sight both of our humanity as such and of the richness of
human plurality, not to speak of the recognition that all are
sinners in need of grace and forgiveness.

Let us refract this a little further by way of a specific example that, in our society, has generated much rights talk and
indeed rights litigation – namely, gender. The question about
gender that we left hanging earlier needs to be addressed in
a more nuanced way.[11] Are men and women to be regarded

---

11 The question of race needs a separate treatment, which I will not
   attempt here.

(1) as by definition a superior and an inferior, or (2) as identical in all important respects, or (3) as analogical beings who work out their distinct identities in relation to one another? The first represents a long-standing (pre-Christian) tradition, now generally abandoned; the second is the view to which the nominalist approach has tended; the third is the view that most comports with Roman Catholic understandings of rights and with the anthropology that undergirds it – though here of course we part company with those of our Christian forebears who also tried to see in the male the most perfect representation of what it means to be created in the image of God.[12]

Why the third and not the second? The second view, on close inspection, does not do justice to our humanity. It reflects the fact that rights talk has been driven more and more into a Machiavellian modus operandi, that it is has become a way to get and to hold power through a harsh politicization of all human relationships. This has required the flattening out of male/female differences such that neither gender is properly respected in its own right. It has undermined the dialogical relation between men and women as co-creators and sustainers of one another, under the aegis of a transcendent Creator and Sustainer, knowledge of whom brings an appropriate humility to all human projects.

The third view, on the other hand, draws into a single frame of reference rights as markers of human dignity and a view of male and female that respects both their distinctiveness and their mutual dependence. Not every problem is thereby resolved, of course; but a theological basis for understanding rights is proffered in a way that provides ample ground for

---

12 Sr. Prudence Allen notes that John Paul II "states explicitly that woman and man equally reflect the image of God." It is hard, she says, "to overestimate the significance of this shift in emphasis and what it is bringing to the Church's understanding of man and woman as persons" ("Integral Sex Complementarity and the Theology of Communion," *Communio* 17, Winter 1990, 542f.).

disputation over the implications of this view for male and female standing, offices, and identities.[13]

Rights, understood as markers of human dignity, cannot be deployed as vehicles of conquest and domination unless human dignity itself is understood in terms of conquest and domination. That is a view of human dignity, popularized by nominalists and their heirs, that is foreign to Roman Catholic social teaching, which takes it cue first of all from the incarnation and passion of Jesus Christ. Rights are the way we chasten dominion in the present age, limiting as far as possible the disordering of human life and the repression of human dignity through sinful rapacity and greed.

RIGHTS, GOODS, AND GOD

Thus we are borne full circle back to our central imperatives. The ends towards which rights tend cannot be evaluated apart from a recognition of human fragility and vulnerability, but something more is required. The Universal Declaration of Human Rights rightly affirms the "inherent dignity" of all persons. This dignity is not free-floating; and, if it is to undergird and to sustain human rights principles, then this affirmation cannot be free-floating either. Human dignity is lodged in the fact that human beings are creatures of a certain sort, creatures in fact who derive their dignity directly from God, whose personhood is a capacity for communion with God.

Roman Catholic social teaching recognizes this and tries to take its bearings from it. To quote once more from John Paul II:

---

13 In his 1994 World Day of Peace message, John Paul II offered reflections on "Women: Teachers of Peace." His starting point was clear: "If, from the very beginning, girls are looked down upon or regarded as inferior, their sense of dignity will be gravely impaired and their healthy development inevitably compromised. Discrimination in childhood will have lifelong effects and will prevent women from fully taking part in the life of society." The ground here is an ontology of human dignity that yields strong conclusions against invidious comparisons and ill use.

"Truly, one must recognize that, with an unstoppable crescendo from the Old to the New Testament, there is manifested in Christianity the authentic conception of man as a person and no longer merely as an individual. If an individual perishes, the species remains unaltered: in the logic established by Christianity, however, when a person dies, something unique and unrepeatable is lost."[14] If contemporary Western society, for its part, has difficulty findings its bearings in human rights discourse – if it has difficulty figuring out an intelligible and defensible way to articulate the contours of human rights and to discipline or limit rights discourse – that is in part because it has embraced a nominalist construal of the problem. That construal admits of pragmatic adjudication only, avoiding the most crucial questions about human dignity. It thus affords poor guidance both about what should count as an offence or act of violence and about what is a basic entitlement.

In "Human Rights: The Midlife Crisis," Michael Ignatieff points out that a cloak of silence has been "thrown over the question of God." Ignatieff's reference point is the deliberations that led to the Universal Declaration itself. In Ignatieff's words: "The Universal Declaration enunciates rights; it doesn't explain why people have them." Communist and some non-Communist delegations, at the time of the drafting, rejected explicitly any reference to human beings as created in God's image. Even the fortifying qualification, "by nature," failed to pass muster. So, concludes Ignatieff, "secularism has become the lingua franca of global human rights, as English has become the *lingua franca* of the global economy. Both serve as lowest common denominators, enabling people to pretend to share more than they actually do."[15]

---

14 See Filibeck, *Human Rights in the Teaching of the Church,* 51.

15 *New York Review of Books,* 20 May 1999, 58. Ignatieff recounts an amusing tale about an incident that occurred when "Eleanor Roosevelt first convened a drafting committee in her Washington Square apartment in February, 1947." Apparently, a "Chinese Confucian and a Lebanese Thomist got into such an argument

Can this pretence be kept up? Or will it lead in time to a grave deterioration of the culture of rights? We cannot predict the future with great confidence, perhaps. Ignatieff, for one, is undaunted for it is none too clear to him "why human rights need the idea of the sacred at all." Why, he asks, "do we need an idea of God in order to believe that human beings should not be beaten, tortured, coerced, indoctrinated, or in any way sacrificed against their will?" This conviction, he insists, derives from a certain version of moral reciprocity, a secularized Golden Rule. He calls this a minimalist anthropology. But just how reliable is such a notion of moral reciprocity absent a substantive notion of persons and their moral standing?[16]

What sort of human rights culture are we building? To give the answer to that question we need to be able to give an answer, however tentative or clear, to several other questions as well: What is a human person? What is the nature and source of human dignity? In what human goods do we really believe? Do rights have an organizing principle? Do rights require God? It may be that the fate of a Soon Ok Lee, or of others like her, hangs on our response.

---

about the philosophical and metaphysical bases of rights that Mrs. Roosevelt concluded that the only way forward lay in the West and East agreeing to disagree" (58). If anything, the urge to refrain from tackling the question of justification is even more exigent now, given contemporary and often ardent multiculturalist realities and ideologies.

16 I do not mean to imply that this substantive notion is a correlative of religion simply as such. Certainly it cannot be taken for granted in any and every context where God or gods are confessed. It was not operative, for example, to take an extreme case, in Taliban-dominated Afghanistan; nor has it always been operative on a consistent basis even where one might reasonably expect to find it.

6

Considering Secularism

IAIN T. BENSON

One good reason for troubling to concentrate on the moment of change of meaning is that it directs our attention – awakens us – to fundamental assumptions so deeply held that no one even thinks of making them explicit.

– *Owen Barfield*

FOR WANT OF JUDICIAL CONSIDERATION

In a recent decision the majority judges of the Supreme Court of Canada determined that the common usage of "secular" to indicate "non-religious" is, for the purposes of law, erroneous.[1] The court held that the secular sphere must not be deemed to exclude religion and must allow scope for consciences animated by religious conviction as well as those that are not.[2] Its

---

1 *Chamberlain v. Surrey School District No. 36* [2002] 4 S.C.R. 710 (*"Chamberlain"*).

2 Various commentators have been critical of the approach to the definition of "secular" accepted by the Supreme Court of Canada and the British Columbia Court of Appeal. Two academics, in attempts to influence the former through articles put into argument before it, affirmed a religion-exclusive conception, arguing that this satisfied "justificatory neutrality." See Bruce MacDougall, "A Respectful Distance: Appellate Courts Consider Religious Motivation

reasoning in this decision is compatible with the following analytical framework: though the secular overlaps with the religious, the secular state does not have jurisdiction over the religions, just as the religions, though they are active in the public sphere, do not have jurisdiction over the state. In this sense, church and state are indeed separate, but that does not mean, as much anti-religious sentiment has it, that the state cannot cooperate with religions. Religious believers have as much right as anyone else to function in society according to their beliefs; likewise, religious institutions have as much right as non-religious institutions. Religious belief and identification ought not, on this reading, to function as a liability within a free and democratic society. Everyone has a belief system of some sort, and those who draw on religious sources should not be put at a disadvantage. Arguments based upon claims of neutrality, then, in so far as they amount to veiled attempts to exclude religious conceptions from public life, are no longer those that should dominate judicial interpretation.

These are the main implications of the reconceptualizing of the secular that occurred in the Supreme Court of Canada's *Chamberlain* decision. In coming to a religion-inclusive view of the secular, the court followed a unanimous panel of the British Columbia Court of Appeal, which had overturned a trial judge who had found that the term "secular principles" required that decisions made by elected school trustees, if based "even in part" on religious convictions, should be quashed. However, in what might be called *obiter* comments, the seven judges of the majority (in two separate sets of written reasons) stated that Canada is based on the principles of secularism. And that too is important to notice.

---

of Public Figures in Homosexual Equality Discourse – The Cases of Chamberlain and Trinity Western University," *UBC Law Review* 35 (2002): 511–38; and John Russell, "How to Be Fair to Religious and Secular Ideals within the Liberal State," *The Advocate* 60, 3 (2002): 345–58. Neither were found persuasive by the court.

The *Chamberlain* case required the court to examine the phrase "strictly secular and non-sectarian" in the School Act of British Columbia. That act, however, did not use the term "secularism." While it was necessary to examine the term "secular," it was not necessary to discuss "secularism," and the definition of the latter was not argued before the court. What I want to argue here, with respect, is that the majority judges of the Supreme Court of Canada erred in their use of the term "secularism" because they did not stop to consider that the ideology of secularism (first articulated by G.J. Holyoake in mid-nineteenth-century England) is inconsistent with the court's own view of the secular. In equating "secular" with "secularism" the majority judges overlooked the fact that, at its historic origins, the intention of secularism was precisely to exclude religion from all public aspects of society – the very thing the court itself refused to do.

Simply put: the Supreme Court of Canada failed to recognize that the term "secularism" describes an ideology that is, and has been since its inception, anti-religious. As such, the ideology of secularism cannot be one of the principles upon which Canada, as a free and democratic country, is based. Both the judiciary and society at large need to come to clarity on this point, as I hope to show.

THE SECULARISM OF
GEORGE JACOB HOLYOAKE

Consider the following definition of secularism from the *Encyclopaedia Brittanica*, eleventh edition:

Secularism [is] a term applied specially ... to the system of social ethics associated with the name of G.J. Holyoake (*q.v.*). As the word implies, secularism is based solely on considerations of practical morality with a view to the physical, social and moral improvements of society. It neither affirms nor denies the theistic premises of religion, and is thus a particular variety of utilitarianism. Holyoake founded a society in London which subsequently under the leadership of Charles Bradlaugh advocated the disestablishment of the

Church, the abolition of the Second Chamber and other political
and economic reforms.[3]

So matters stood, apparently, in 1911, when the above definition was published. Secularism was seen as a variety of the
utilitarianism that had grown up alongside it rather than as
something specifically anti-religious. But the *Oxford English
Dictionary* informs us that the term was coined by Holyoake
(c. 1851), and Holyoake's views warrant closer examination.

Among the governing ideas listed by the National Secular
Society, founded by Holyoake in 1866, is this: "We assert that
supernaturalism is based upon ignorance and is the historic
enemy of progress."[4] Turning to his own major work, *English
Secularism: A Confession of Belief*, we quickly discover the inac-
curacy of *Brittanica*'s claim – lifted, though it was, directly from
the book – that secularism "neither affirms nor denies the
theistic premises of religion." Extolling the liberation of
humanity by the exercise of reason, Holyoake writes: "Self-
regarding criticism having discovered the insufficiency of theology for the guidance of man, next sought to ascertain what
rules human reason may supply for the independent conduct
of life, which is the object of Secularism." Secularists, he says,
claim to have found truth, at least "so much as replaces the

---

3 P. 573.

4 Editor's note: The National Secular Society identifies Charles
   Bradlaugh (1833–1891) as its official founder, but its Web site
   contains the following remarks, quoting from one Ian G. Andrews
   (<www.secularism.org.uk>, 17 January 2003): "It would seem appropriate that any 'Heroes of Atheism' Poll should include the
   man who coined the term Secularism. He was George Jacob
   Holyoake, born in Birmingham in 1817. Although Charles Bradlaugh established the National Secular Society, Holyoake did the
   groundwork in the decade or so before 1866. Holyoake is the link
   between the old radicalism of Paine, Owen and the Chartists, and
   the Victorian Radicals, such as Bradlaugh."

chief errors and uncertainties of theology." In setting out the essential principles of secularism, he states that it is "a code of duty pertaining to this life, founded on considerations purely human, and intended mainly for those who find theology indefinite or inadequate, unreliable or unbelievable."[5]

His subtitle notwithstanding, Holyoake attempts to stake out a high ground that is "beyond speculation," which he says is the limitation of both the atheist and the theist.

Though respecting the right of the atheist and theist to their theories of the origin of nature, the Secularist regards them as belonging to the debatable ground of speculation. Secularism neither asks nor gives any opinion upon them, confining itself to the entirely independent field of study – the order of the universe. Neither asserting nor denying theism or a future life, having no sufficient reason to give if called upon; the fact remains that material influences exist, vast and available for good, as men have the will and wit to employ them. Whatever may be the value of metaphysical or theological theories of morals, utility in conduct is a daily test of common sense, and is capable of deciding intelligently more questions of practical duty than any other rule. Considerations which pertain to the general welfare, operate without the machinery of theological creeds, and over masses of men in every land to whom Christian incentives are alien, or disregarded.[6]

For Holyoake the order of the universe is ascertainable by the unaided human reason and requires no reference to the God question or to the question of life after death. But this bold confession can hardly be made without at the same time denying that the universe is ordered by and to a Creator.

Whether or not the secularist's confession is beyond speculation, it is certainly not beyond assertion or denial where religion is concerned. Under the rubric "Rejected Tenets

---

5 Holyoake, *English Secularism*, 34f.

6 Ibid., 37.

Replaced by Better," Holyoake invites the reader to "suppose
that criticism has established" the following:

1 That God is unknown.
2 That a future life is unprovable.
3 That the Bible is not a practical guide.
4 That Providence sleeps.
5 That prayer is futile.
6 That original sin is untrue.
7 That eternal perdition is unreal.

Secularist truth, he insists, "should tread close upon the heels
of theological error" so as to counteract and remedy it. Thus,
for example, "for the providence of Scripture, Secularism
directs men to the providence of science, which provides
against peril, or brings deliverance when peril comes." Instead
of "futile prayer," secularism proposes "self-help and the
employment of all the resources of manliness and industry."
Instead of belief in "original depravity," secularism aims to
"promote the moralisation of this world which Christianity has
proved ineffectual to accomplish."[7]

That Holyoake views secularism as a substitute for religion
is clear enough. Secularism provides a superior ethical system
for society, with a much broader appeal.

None of the earlier critics of Secularism, as has been said (and not
many in the later years), realised that it was addressed, not to
Christians, but to those who rejected Christianity, or who were indifferent to it, and were outside it. Christians cannot do anything to
inspire *them* with ethical principles, since they do not believe in
morality unless based on their supernatural tenets. They have to
convert men to Theism, to miracles, prophecy, inspiration of the
Scriptures, the Trinity, and other soul-wearying doctrines, before
they can inculcate morality they can trust. We do not rush in where
they fear to tread. Secularism moves where they do not tread at all.[8]

---

7 Ibid., 71–3.
8 Ibid., 82 f. (emphasis in original).

The secularist policy is "to accept the purely moral teaching of the Bible, and to controvert its theology, in such respects as it contradicts and discourages ethical effort."[9] In this way, it may hope to wean the more sensible away from the errors of Christianity: "True respect would treat God as though at least he is a gentlemen [sic]. Christianity does not do this. No gentleman would accept thanks for benefits he had not conferred, nor would he exact thanks daily and hourly for gifts he had really made, nor have the vanity to covet perpetual thanksgivings. He who would respect God, or respect himself, must seek a faith apart from such Christianity."[10] Secularism's desire is to "convert churches and chapels into temples of instruction for the people ... to solicit priests to be teachers of useful knowledge."[11]

As if to highlight the nature of secularism as an alternative to religion, Holyoake ends his book with proposals for "secularist ceremonies" as he recognizes that ceremonies should be consistent with the opinions of those in whose names they take place. These include ceremonies for marriage, the naming of children, and the death of children; and a vocational admonition encouraging "a career of public usefulness." Supported by numerous Victorian quotations of the type "every man should do his duty in the face of life's vicissitudes," Holyoake approaches his final – empirically unverifiable – certainty, that "between the cradle and the grave is the whole existence of man."[12]

In sum, it would seem that secularism is not properly described as "neither affirming nor denying theism."[13] Holyoake himself denies theism root and branch, as we have seen. Yet this disingenuous description has been thoughtlessly and uncritically echoed, even by otherwise reliable sources like *Britannica*,

---

9 Ibid., 91.

10 Ibid., 103.

11 Ibid., 119.

12 Ibid., 141; see 126ff.

13 Ibid., 37.

down to the present time.[14] Today we might call it the claim
to liberal neutrality. And in this way much of the language
relating to the secular has quietly been steered in an anti-
religious direction. Take the word "secularization," for example, which is commonly defined as "the process in which religious consciousness, activities and institutions lose social
significance. It indicates that religion becomes marginal to the
operation of the social system, and that the essential functions
for the operation of society become rationalized, passing out
of the control of agencies devoted to the supernatural."[15] Such
a definition obscures the anti-religious dimension of secularism by describing its results without reference to their cause –
for ideological secularism is indeed prominent among the
causes of the process here indicated. Moreover, it falsely
suggests that this process is both natural and inevitable.[16]

Not all secularism announces itself in Holyoake's stark
terms. Yet it simply will not do to overlook the anti-religious
aspects and associations of secularism.[17] With this in mind, let

14 Compare, for example, the *Oxford English Reference Dictionary* (2nd
    rev. ed., 2002). See further my "The Secular: Hidden and Express
    Meanings," *Sacred Web* 9 (2002): 125–39; and "Notes Towards a
    (Re)Definition of the 'Secular'" *UBC Law Review* 33 (2000): 519–
    49. Christine L. Niles also challenges the epistemology of a "faith-
    free" notion of the secular in "Epistemological Nonsense? The
    Secular/Religious Distinction," *Notre Dame Journal of Law, Ethics
    and Public Policy* 17 (2003): 561–92.
15 B.R. Wilson, "Secularization," in Eliade, *The Encyclopedia of
    Religion,* 15: 160.
16 As John Finnis observes: "Neither the differentiating of the secu-
    lar from the sacred, nor the social processes of secularization,
    entail the mind-set or cluster of ideologies we call 'secularism.'"
    See his "On the Practical Meaning of Secularism," *Notre Dame Law
    Review* 73 (1998): 492. In this light, see also Casanova, *Public
    Religions in the Modern World.*
17 Compare Kathleen Sullivan, "Religion and Liberal Democracy,"
    University of Chicago Law Review 59 (1992): 197 (cited by Niles,
    "Epistemological Nonsense, 577, n. 62).

us return to the question of how the terms "secular" and "secularism" have been employed in recent decisions of the Canadian courts.

DEVELOPING A MORE INCLUSIVE VIEW OF THE SECULAR

Chief Justice Lamer began his dissent in the *Rodriguez* case, in which the Criminal Code prohibition of physician-assisted suicide was upheld by a five to four majority, by noting that the Charter "has established the essentially secular nature of Canadian society and the central place of freedom of conscience in the operation of our institutions."[18] The grounds for such a statement are not clear. But what, in any case, does it mean for a country to have an essentially secular nature? The passage suggests only that an affirmation of the secular nature of the country is necessary to preserve "the central place of freedom of conscience in the operation of our institutions." And this in turn is linked to questions of religious freedom. Chief Justice Lamer here cites his predecessor, Chief Justice Dickson, in the seminal case, *R. v. Big M Drug Mart*: "The essence of the concept of freedom of religion is the right to entertain such religious beliefs as a person chooses, the right to declare religious beliefs openly and without fear of hindrance or reprisal, and the right to manifest religious belief by worship and practice or by teaching and dissemination."[19] Freedom of religion also means that the state cannot coerce an individual to affirm a specific religious belief or to manifest a specific religious practice. Thus in the *Big M* decision

18 *Rodriguez v. British Columbia (AG)* [1993] 107 D.L.R. (4th) 342, p. 366. A review of the preamble to the Charter, and of the court's affirmation of "religious tradition" as one of the interpretive aspects of a proper contextual approach in Charter cases (this by the majority judges in *Egan* 1995), already raises doubts about the validity of this claim.

19 *R. v. Big M Drug Mart Ltd.* [1985] 1 S.C.R. 295 ("Big M"), p. 336.

against Sunday-closing legislation, it was fatal that the legislation had a religiously based purpose and could therefore be seen as coercive of those who were not religious. When later legislation was challenged, it survived on the basis that its purpose had become "secular."[20]

This was the state of play prior to December 2002, when the Supreme Court issued its reasons in *Chamberlain*. Until that point it had not defined "secular" with any precision or clarity, but it was now faced with an examination of the phrase "strictly secular and non-sectarian." The particulars of the case merit our attention: three books showing same-sex parents were the subject of an application for approval as classroom resource materials in a public school. The matter came for approval before the locally elected trustees of the school district. The school board trustees refused to approve the books, and various people, including members of a gay advocacy group, petitioned the court to set aside the trustees' decision. Madam Justice Saunders, at the trial of the matter, held that the trustees' resolution breached a requirement of the School Act which provides that all schools "shall be conducted on strictly secular and non-sectarian principles."[21] She held that the school board had breached this statutory requirement because "the words 'conducted on strictly secular principles' preclude a decision *significantly influenced by religious considerations*."[22] For this judge, then, the requirement

---

20 Any effect on Saturday-observing consumers, say, could thus survive a sec. 1 analysis, which allows infringements of rights to be upheld as long as they represent "such reasonable limits, prescribed by law, as can be demonstrably justified in a free and democratic society."

21 The section reads: "Conduct 76.(1) All schools and Provincial schools must be conducted on strictly secular and non-sectarian principles; (2) The highest morality must be inculcated, but no religious dogma or creed is to be taught in a school or Provincial school."

22 Ibid., 330 (emphasis added).

that a public body function on secular principles meant that no concerns in education may be influenced by or based upon religious belief.

When the case went to the British Columbia Court of Appeal, it was argued that Madam Justice Saunders' interpretation of the term "secular principles" was erroneous since it placed the beliefs of religious citizens at a disadvantage vis-à-vis the beliefs of non-religious citizens. The argument was successful. Writing for the unanimous panel of the Court of Appeal, Justice McKenzie analyzed the term "secular" in a manner that, for the first time, looked behind the term and considered the results of alternative interpretations. In doing so, the court adopted an approach to the secular that includes, rather than excludes, religion: "A religiously informed conscience should not be accorded any privilege, *but neither should it be placed under a disability.* In a truly free society moral positions advance or retreat in their influence on law and public policy through decisions of public officials who are not required to pass a religious litmus test."[23]

When the appeal from this decision went to the Supreme Court of Canada, one of the arguments advanced by counsel for the appellant was that the approach to the "secular" taken by the Court of Appeal was itself misguided. The Supreme Court disagreed, as we have already seen. Though it overturned the British Columbia Court of Appeal in the result (remitting the matter back to the school trustees for reconsideration), it left untouched that court's finding on the religion-inclusive secular. All nine justices upheld the Court of Appeal with respect to "religious considerations" being valid aspects

---

23 *Chamberlain v. Surrey School Board* (2000), 80 B.C.L.R. (3d) 181 (C.A.), *per* McKenzie J.A. (par. 28, emphasis added); reversing (1998) 60 B.C.L.R. (3d) 311 (S.C.). A more detailed analysis of this decision, written by Brad Miller and myself, can be found on *LexView* (<www.centreforrenewal.ca>).

of a determination under the rubric "secular" in the School
Act of British Columbia.[24]

What then are we to make of the fact that the same court that
accepted the religion-inclusive use of "secular" failed to reckon
with the ideological nature of "secularism"? Prior to *Chamberlain*,
judges often used "secular" in its common but philosophically
unsound sense, without considering alternative interpretations.
Will they now continue to do so with respect to the term "secularism"? With what effects? The manner in which the majority judges analyzed the case suggests that real confusion persists
and that it is not confined to the level of semantics but, rather,
touches on core issues of religious freedom, the nature of

---

24 Since the chief justice expressly agreed with the manner in which
    the dissenting judges addressed the question of the secular, their
    approach can be said to be the opinion of the court on the ques-
    tion. In his dissent Gonthier J. writes at par. 137: "In my view,
    Saunders J. below erred in her assumption that 'secular' effective-
    ly meant 'non-religious.' This is incorrect since nothing in the
    Charter, political or democratic theory, or a proper understanding
    of pluralism demands that atheistically based moral positions
    trump religiously based moral positions on matters of public pol-
    icy. I note that the preamble to the *Charter* itself establishes that
    '... Canada is founded upon principles that recognize the su-
    premacy of God and the rule of law.' According to the reasoning
    espoused by Saunders J., if one's moral view manifests from a
    religiously grounded faith, it is not to be heard in the public
    square, but if it does not, then it is publicly acceptable. The prob-
    lem with this approach is that everyone has 'belief' or 'faith' in
    something, be it atheistic, agnostic or religious. To construe the
    'secular' as the realm of the 'unbelief' is therefore erroneous.
    Given this, why, then, should the religiously informed conscience
    be placed at a public disadvantage or disqualification? To do so
    would be to distort liberal principles in an illiberal fashion and
    would provide only a feeble notion of pluralism. The key is that
    people will disagree about important issues, and such disagree-
    ment, where it does not imperil community living, must be capa-
    ble of being accommodated at the core of a modern pluralism."

pluralism, and the principles that govern public policy. Their own analysis shows more than one persistent trace of ideologically exclusive secularism, not least where it implies that the religious views of parents must be subordinated to the overriding liberal values of "tolerance" and "diversity."[25]

A NEW LIBERALISM?

In a perceptive article entitled "Secular Fundamentalism," Paul Campos observes that many secularists appear blind to the way in which their conception of liberal principles and values poses a threat to genuine diversity. Referring to the prevailing Rawlsian vision of liberalism, Campos writes:

The irony, of course, is that in this triumphalistic incarnation liberalism can begin to resemble the very dogmatic systems that it once rebelled against. Despite its highly abstract endorsement of moral and religious pluralism, [John Rawls's] *Political Liberalism* is ultimately a paean to a secular creed that has within it the potential to become every bit as monistic, compulsory, and intolerant of any significant deviation from social verities as the traditional modes of belief it derided and displaced.[26]

---

25 The majority view is summarized by McLachlin C.J. at par. 25: "In summary, the Act's requirement of strict secularism [*sic*] means that the Board must conduct its deliberations on all matters, including the approval of supplementary resources, in a manner that respects the views of all members of the school community. It cannot prefer the religious views of some people in its district to the views of other segments of the community. *Nor can it appeal to views that deny the equal validity of the lawful lifestyles of some in the school community.* The Board must act in a way that promotes respect and tolerance for all the diverse groups that it represents and serves" (emphasis added).

26 Paul F. Campos, "Secular Fundamentalism," *Columbia Law Review* 94 (1994): 1825. (Thanks to Professor Ian Leigh of the Department of Law, Durham University, for bringing this article to my attention.)

What is the remedy to this new dogmatism, which preaches tolerance but practises intolerance? Which regards itself as liberal but is too often illiberal?

The British philosopher John Gray, who also cautions us to beware the monistic counterfeits of tolerance and diversity, argues that authentic liberalism must eschew all approaches that foresee a common end point to societal evolution.[27] According to Gray, if we are to do justice to our actual diversity, then we will need a different sort of liberal philosophy than the one to which we are accustomed. Liberalism, he says, may take two forms:

In one, toleration is justified as a means to truth. In this view toleration is an instrument of rational consensus, and a diversity of ways of life is endured in the faith that it is destined to disappear. In the other, toleration is valued as a condition of peace, and divergent ways of living are welcomed as marks of diversity in the good life. The first conception supports an ideal of ultimate convergence on values, the latter an ideal of *modus vivendi*. Liberalism's future lies in turning its face away from the ideal of rational consensus and looking instead to *modus vivendi*.[28]

Gray, I think, is largely right. The good news for Canada is that some of the seeds for the new liberalism, that is, for the modus vivendi envisioned by Gray, can be found in the refiguring of

---

27 Recall here the National Secular Society's principle: "We assert that supernaturalism is based upon ignorance and is the historic enemy of progress."

28 Gray, *Two Faces of Liberalism*, 105, continues: "The predominant liberal view of toleration sees it as a means to a universal civilization. If we give up this view, and welcome a world that contains many ways of life and regimes, we will have to think afresh about human rights and democratic government. We will refashion these inheritances to serve a different liberal philosophy. We will come to think of human rights as convenient articles of peace, whereby individuals and communities with conflicting values and interests may consent to coexist." (I am indebted to Peter Lauwers for introducing me to Gray's important work.)

"the secular" that occurred in the *Chamberlain* decision. But these seeds will be nurtured into fruition if, and only if, the monistic tendencies of the older liberalism, influenced as it is by a history of anti-religious secularism, are still more decisively abandoned.

Can our judges and politicians extricate law and public policy from the rocky soil of that secularism and from the terrain of a liberalism that is inhospitable to genuine tolerance and diversity? Certainly the early decades of Charter jurisprudence suggest that extrication will not be an easy task. So does the *Chamberlain* case itself. Its confusion about secularism led to practical results that did not so much uphold diversity as undermine it. Contrary to the court's own principles, the *Chamberlain* decision produced a rank-ordering of rights in which the sexual dogma of same-sex advocates effectively trumped all challengers, including those of parents with religious convictions about their children's education.[29] That,

---

29 In *Dagenais v. Canadian Broadcasting Corporation* [1994] 3 S.C.R. 835, we read at par. 31: "When the protected rights of two individuals come into conflict ... *Charter* principles require a balance to be achieved that fully respects the importance of both sets of rights." Only the dissenting judges refer to *Dagenais*, however. In the two sets of reasons given for the majority opinion, the thought process is quite different. Both the chief justice and Justice LeBel rely on the general concept of Charter values rather than any particular Charter right; that is why words like "diversity" and "tolerance" are elevated to near constitutional significance. Moreover, when they deal with the equality rights provision, they fail to draw attention to the fact that religion is actually listed there, unlike the judicially "embodied" protection for sexual orientation. (Though the latter was deliberately left out of sec. 15 – see the Proceedings of the Joint Committee of the Senate and House of Commons [1981] 48, 33f. – it was later found to be analogous to the listed terms, and in 1995 was read in by the Supreme Court in *Egan and Nesbit*.) So we are not altogether surprised when sexual orientation is somehow found to be a weightier concern than religion. But that contravenes both the court's own proscription against rank-ordering of Charter rights and the language of the provision itself.

of course, is a sign of the old secularism – or should we say, with Graham Good, "the new sectarianism"? – at work.[30] It cannot be denied that, at the moment, the Supreme Court of Canada's endorsement of secularism as a Canadian constitutional principle is in stark contradiction to its religion-inclusive use of the word "secular."

30 Compare Graham, *Humanism Betrayed*, chap. 2.

7

Birth, Death, and Technoscience

Searching for Values
at the Margins of Life

MARGARET SOMERVILLE

THE CHANGING CONTEXT OF
BIRTH AND DEATH

We humans have always formed our most important values
and sought meaning in life by weaving a metaphorical fabric
around the two marker events of every human life: birth and
death. Our perceptions of birth, and the values traditionally
attached to it, are being challenged and changed, however, by
the new technoscience. The "new genetics" debate is the context in which that is occurring. There is also a companion
debate about euthanasia,[1] focusing on the values that should
govern death. While euthanasia is not a new issue, the current
debate is of a different order (it is widespread in Western
democracies) and possibly different in kind (it is based on
individual rights) from those in the past. It is not an accident
that we are presently debating both *eu-genics* (good at birth)
and *eu-thanasia* (good at death) because the substance of these
two debates is linked in many ways. Consequently, what we

---

1 Throughout this text I use the word "euthanasia" to include
physician-assisted suicide. In some circumstances, not relevant
here, they must be differentiated.

decide in terms of ethics and law in one of them is likely to have an impact on the other.

Reprogenetics[2] has faced us with unprecedented possibilities regarding "birth," such as the passing on of human life through cloning. Such technologies challenge our traditional values and make us aware of a values void, at least at a societal level[3] – whether that void exists because we no longer agree on the values that should apply or because the situation is so novel that we do not have immediately apparent values to govern it.

Just twenty-five years ago we were stunned by the birth of Louise Brown, the first test-tube baby. Today in vitro fertilization (IVF) is routine medical practice. Now we face the advent of technologies much more radical than IVF. They do not merely try, as does IVF, to repair nature when it fails; rather, they try to make possible what, in nature, is impossible. As well as cloning, these technologies include: creating embryos from three or more genetic parents or, in the future, from two ova or two sperm; using human embryos as repair kits for ourselves (e.g., to make replacement organs or tissues); and choosing the characteristics of our children. Should we just allow individuals and the market to decide which of these technologies will be used and how – an approach based on a combination of intense individualism and market-place ethics? Or should we as a society draw lines that must not be crossed? If so, where should they be drawn?

That is where we do not agree. And in a pluralistic, multi-cultural, secular, postmodern, democratic society such as Canada, it is unlikely that we will find such agreement. But we do not have a "no values" option; choosing not to articulate or defend any values is itself a values choice. In short, *some* societal values will govern these technologies, even though we do not all agree on them. The same is true for the values that

---

2 That is, reproductive technologies and genetics.

3 See my "Ethics and Architects: Spaces, Voids, and Travelling-in-Hope," Pelleteir and Pérez-Gomez, *Architecture, Ethics and Technology*, 61–79.

will govern human death. What process, then, should we use
to determine these values? It is likely that we will also disagree
in that regard.

Finding shared values in the contemporary public square is
a very complex process. It requires careful research to develop
ethical and just approaches to finding these values. These
approaches must foster an ethics of complexity that will allow
us to take into account the claims and needs of both individuals and society; different cultures and world views; and a
range of (sometimes conflicting) understandings of human
nature, of the human-nature relationship, and of what it means
to be human. We are only at the very beginning of developing
such an ethics.

One common mistake in searching for values, and for the
process that should be used to establish them at the societal
level, deserves mention: equating morality and ethics with
democracy. Democracy is morally and ethically neutral: it is
only as ethical as the voters and their elected representatives
make it. A majority of Canadians voting in favour of, for example, creating human embryos in order to use them for stem
cell research, or in favour of euthanasia, does not mean that
these practices are morally and ethically acceptable. One
cannot do ethics by majority vote. Indeed, current computer-
based research in the philosophy of science demonstrates the
impact and importance of even just a few voices crying in the
ethical wilderness. Very large decision-making sets (for
instance, 5,000 or 10,000 consecutive decisions), where one
group of participants decides to act ethically and the other
unethically, show that, as long as a small nucleus of ethical
decision makers remains, ethics can survive and eventually
flourish even when the vast majority of people act unethically.
But if those few voices are lost, so too is ethics.[4] That is both
a very sobering and a very hopeful message.

---

4 J. Bigelow, "Simpson's Paradox and the Selfish Universal," paper
  presented at the Australasian Association for History, Philosophy,
  and Social Studies of Science Conference, Melbourne, 2001.

HUMAN DIGNITY AND RESPECT FOR LIFE

Respect for human dignity is often put forward as the primary value that should govern both birth and death. In the twenty-first century that translates into the values that should govern the new genetics and the decision about legalizing euthanasia. But there are dangers, not always recognized, in using this concept. There are two versions of the concept of dignity – intrinsic human dignity and extrinsic human dignity – the applications of which can have radically different outcomes.[5] Intrinsic human dignity focuses on the idea that every human being is seen as having innate human dignity, which must be respected. At a minimum, it requires respect for the life of that person. Extrinsic human dignity focuses on the "quality of life" of the person and, if this is perceived to be below a certain level, the person is regarded as lacking dignity. Proposals to remedy situations of a perceived lack of dignity include, for instance, discarding human embryos with a genetic "abnormality" (such as Down syndrome) or euthanizing persons who are terminally ill. In both cases the idea is to respect such dignity as these humans may be deemed to have. But that is to accept that life itself is an affront to their dignity and, therefore, that eliminating them does not contravene their dignity. Indeed, it implements respect for it.[6]

Concepts such as human dignity and quality of life were originally formulated in order to protect human life. They provided a basis for people's claims that they had a right to be treated in certain ways or to receive certain care or treatment; denial of such treatment would amount to a failure to respect their dignity or to fulfill an obligation to ensure a minimally adequate quality of life. In contemporary society, however, the

---

5 See Somerville, *Death Talk*. See also S.D. Stolberg, "Human Dignity and Disease, Disability, Suffering: A Philosophical Contribution to the Euthanasia and Assisted Suicide Debate," *Humane Medicine* 11 (1995): 144–7.

6 See further Somerville, *Ethical Canary*, 29f.

concepts are often used to the opposite effect – to argue, for example, that a person's quality of life is so low that it does not merit either protection or the cost of support, or that continuing to live is an affront to the person's dignity and therefore his or her life should be ended. The notion of *intrinsic* human dignity cannot be used in this way, however; it requires respect for all humans and for human life as such.

Because of the ambiguity of the concept of respect for human dignity and its potential for misuse, we should not use it as a substitute for the concept of respect for human life, although it can have value when used as a secondary or back-up concept to the latter. What, then, does respect for human life require of us?

CHALLENGES TO TRADITIONAL RESPECT FOR LIFE

In the past, respect for life meant largely respect for the life of each individual (although there were exceptions that allowed life to be taken in justified self-defence or defence of others) and respect for human life in general. Such respect remains essential to the protection of both individuals and society and must be upheld at both the individual and societal level. But the new technoscience challenges even this old concept of respect for life.

We are a society that has adopted an intense individualism.[7] In the context of reproduction, that means that people should be free to choose which children they will have and which they will not. Future parent(s) can decide to use technologies such as preimplantation genetic diagnosis (PGD), in which IVF embryos are screened for genetic diseases or abnormalities, or pre-natal screening (including genetic screening) and abortion, to avoid having a child with an unwanted condition.

At an individual level these decisions raise difficult ethical issues. We do not agree on the moral status of the human

---

7 See Fukuyama, *Great Disruption.*

embryo and, consequently, on the respect owed to it. But, if we regard an embryo's life as being entitled to respect, what does that require of us as a society? Does an embryo have a claim to be transferred to a woman's uterus? Does the high rate of failure to implant, or miscarriage of "defective" embryos, offer any justification for allowing them to die? Can we regard a woman's uterus as a life-support treatment for an in vitro embryo and, if so, can we ethically justify not offering it such treatment? What message does discarding embryos because of their defective genes send to members of our society who suffer from the same disability? Does choosing an embryo on the basis of its desired or undesired characteristics turn the embryo into a product or thing? How will the symbolic message created by PGD and pre-natal screening – that the parents want only a child of a certain "quality" and their love is contingent on that being realized – affect the norm that parents' love for their children is unconditional? The flip-side of the parents' love being conditional is that the embryo becomes, to use German philosopher Jürgen Habermas's term, "conditional human life."[8]

Whether or not we can justify PGD and pre-natal screening at the level of individual decision making, collectively these decisions are resulting in an outcome that would never be acceptable as public policy. In reality the new genetics is functioning as eugenics, but that fact is not acknowledged. The cumulative impact of individuals' decisions about reproduction based on preimplantation genetic diagnosis of IVF embryos or prenatal screening of foetuses will be to eliminate certain groups of people – for example, Down syndrome children – from our society. And what other groups might we eliminate? Achondroplastic "dwarf" children? Profoundly deaf children or those with a gene for bipolar (manic-depressive) disorder? To do so would be to wipe out two special cultures in the first two cases and some of our most creative and artistic citizens in the latter.

---

8 See Habermas, *Future of Human Nature.*

To repeat, an outcome that would be unacceptable as a public policy decision – that is, eliminating certain groups of people – is being implemented through the accumulation of individual choices. It is argued in rebuttal that individual choice regarding the nature of one's child is not a eugenic decision, that eugenics is only practised when a choice is made in relation to a group or class of persons and by someone who is not the future parent. But is that not simply sophistry?

At the other end of the life spectrum radical individualism also encourages the view that how one dies is simply a private matter in which no one else – especially not the state or the law – should interfere and that people must therefore be free to choose euthanasia or physician-assisted suicide. But how we die does matter to society and does affect societal values, especially if euthanasia or physician-assisted suicide is involved. Their legalization necessarily requires society's compliance, and their implementation requires the participation of physicians.[9] Consequently, how we die is not just a private matter but, rather, necessitates a number of public policy decisions that establish the norms and values governing what we may and must not do in the context of death. Moreover, if euthanasia were legalized, the collective effect of the decisions of individuals would again have to be taken into account. And what happens to respect for life when, for this reason or that, suicide begins (as in the Netherlands) to become more common – when it becomes, so to say, institutionalized?[10]

It is reprogenetics, however, on which I want to concentrate here. Reprogenetics has faced us with at least three more unprecedented challenges to respect for human life: (1) what does respect for in vitro human embryos require? (2) what does respect for the transmission of human life require? and (3) what does respect for the human germ cell line require?

---

9 D. Callahan, "When Self-Determination Runs Amok," *Hastings Center Report* 22, 2 (1992): 52–5.

10 See Foley and Hendin, *The Case against Assisted Suicide*; and Keown, *Euthanasia, Ethics and Public Policy*.

We are the first humans to face these decisions because we are the first to have the technology that can create the circumstances in which they arise.

Respect for Human Embryos

What does respect for life require of us in relation to the earliest form or stage of life – human embryos – when they exist outside the body of a woman? We face this question because of two major developments: since the mid-seventies we have been creating in vitro human embryos, and, in the last three to five years, they have become of great potential therapeutic and commercial value. Human embryos are a source of stem cells that could be very valuable in making therapeutic products to treat horrible diseases.

That raises a host of questions that include: May we create and kill human embryos in order to use them as the source of therapeutic products? May we clone human embryos for the same purpose? Does the intention involved in creating an embryo matter? Is it unethical to transmit human life to an embryo with the intention of using it as a product but ethical to do so in order to help a woman to have a child? May we use so-called "spare" embryos "left over" from IVF procedures for therapy or research? Is it unethical to use such embryos as commodities but ethical to allow them to die? Or, as some people argue, is it unethical not to use them – that is, to "waste" them? And, if we are going to use human embryos, then is it all right to set up manufacturing plants for that purpose?

The ethical analysis needed to respond to these questions requires, first, an examination of the moral status of the human embryo. There are three current views on this, the practical implications of which range from permissiveness to prohibition:

- The human embryo has no moral status and is equivalent to any other cell or group of cells. It may be treated as we see fit.

- The human embryo is a potential human life. It has moral status and deserves respect but not (yet) the same respect as the rest of us. Therefore it may be used in ways that would not be ethically acceptable if applied to the rest of us.
- The human embryo is a human life with potential – like any other life, or life at any other stage. As the earliest stage of human life, the embryo has the same moral status as the rest of us; after all, we are all ex-embryos. Therefore its life must be respected and it must not be used simply as a product or as a means to an end.

A second and related question also needs to be asked. What impact would using human embryos as products have on our sense, both as individuals and as a society, of what it means to be human and of the nature and meaning of human life?

Jürgen Habermas, in his new book, *The Future of Human Nature*, argues that respect for what he calls pre-personal human life is essential to our ethical self-understanding of humanity as a whole; that is, of what it means to be human.[11] There is an incredible arrogance in an approach based on the idea that our view of a life form – the human embryo – determines its status, worth, and purpose. Moreover,

to the extent that the creation and destruction of embryos for the purposes of medical research are extended and normalized, the cultural perception of antenatal human life will change, too, blunting our moral sensibility for the limits of cost-benefit analyses in general. Today, we are still sensitive to the obscenity of this reifying practice, and wonder whether we want to live in a society which is ready to swap sensitivity regarding the normative and natural foundations of its existence for the narcissistic indulgence of our own preferences.[12]

Then, if we can justify using human embryos to benefit the rest of us, can we, at the other end of the lifespan, also justify

---

11 p. 14.
12 p. 20.

using unconscious, dying people – "neo-morts" – for the same purpose? For instance, may we use them as research subjects, or as subjects upon which physicians-in-training can practise medical interventions, or even, by direct analogy to the use of embryos, as organ or tissue donors? Or would that be a failure to respect human life and human dignity? Many people who would allow the use of human embryos would recoil at the idea of using dying people in such ways. Does that difference in reaction reflect valid moral intuitions regarding the ethical difference between these two situations? Or is it rather a failure to perceive what is needed to respect human life, and to treat it ethically, when we do not personally identify with it because it does not look like us?

Respect for the Transmission of Human Life

Another way in which we must now learn to respect human life is with regard to its mode of transmission. Yet again, we are the first humans to have to consider what that requires. In the past, human life could be transmitted only through sexual intercourse. Although recently there have been scientific reports that it will be more difficult to clone humans than sheep using the "Dolly technique" (somatic cell nuclear transfer [SCNT]),[13] let us assume that it will become possible. Cloning is asexual replication not sexual reproduction. Human cloning can also be carried out using the cells from in vitro human embryos that have not lost their totipotential capacity, which means that each cell can form a new individual – and all are genetically identical. (This same process can occur naturally, resulting in identical twins or triplets. But that does not mean that intentionally cloning embryos in this way is ethically justified. Different ethical considerations apply when we intentionally intervene. Moreover, the natural cloning process is very limited in the number of embryos that can result, whereas

---

13 Margaret Munro, "Humans 'Nearly Impossible' to Clone: Study," *National Post*, 11 April 2003.

the technoscience-assisted cloning process is not.) What must we not do if we are to uphold respect for the transmission of human life?

One school of thought would say there is nothing – beyond, one assumes, what our own conscience might indicate as wrong – that we must not do. In the context of reproduction or replication, intense individualism leads to claims of "a right to absolute reproductive freedom;"[14] that is, to claims that decisions about reproduction are no one else's business (again, especially not the state's business) and that one should be absolutely free to reproduce in whatever way one wishes. Therefore, the argument goes, cloning should not be banned. One should be able to choose a child with one's own genes, just as through PGD or pre-natal screening one can choose not to have a child with certain genetic characteristics.

Whatever else may be said in criticism of the "absolute reproductive freedom" approach, it is plainly to adopt an adult-centred reproductive decision-making model. That is an ethical mistake. The model should be a *child-centred* one, especially when there is a conflict between what is best for the future parents and for the future child. For instance, if adults want to clone themselves, their interests in doing so should not prevail over a child's right not to be created in such a way. The child's interests must prevail, and those interests include not coming into being as a copy of someone else and not being designed by another. We each have a right to our own unique ticket in the great genetic lottery of the passing on of human life. Cloning contravenes that right. A secondary but nevertheless very important objection to cloning is that it carries very serious risks of disease, disability, and a decreased lifespan for the cloned child.

Habermas comes to the same conclusion using a concept that humans have a right not to be "disposed over" – their very

---

14 J.A. Robertson, "Embryos, Families and Procreative Liberty: The Legal Structures of the New Reproduction," *Southern California Law Review* 59 (1986): 939.

essence or nature interfered with – by other humans. He proposes that the contingency of the origins of each of us as
humans is of the essence of being human. We can only truly
become ourself – an authentic person who authors his or her
own life history – if we are free and equal to all others.[15] Both
freedom and equality are compromised if we are designed by
someone else. Cloning is one form of such designing.
Whether we have an absolute right not to have the genetic
inheritance we receive altered is a further question. Certainly,
altering it requires very strong justification, a matter to which
we will return.

Quite apart from the wrong to the future child involved in
cloning, cloning may be deemed a failure of respect for the
transmission of human life since a host of moral objections
arise both in the transition from reproduction to replication
and in the treatment of embryos as "xeroxable"; that is, simply
as products that may be copied. Moreover, even if not deemed
inherently wrong in itself, cloning generates an ethically unacceptable slippery slope. If cloning were allowed, why would it
be permissible to clone one embryo but not ten or even
10,000? And what about the other technoscience modes of
transmission of human life besides cloning: creating an
embryo from two ova or two sperm or three or more genetic
parents, or even, perhaps, from individual genes? Would they
be permissible? Accepting cloning would make it much more
difficult to impose defensible limits on any of these technologies. And lest we think that no more ethically challenging,
mind-altering science than this is possible, what about the
ethics of the rapidly emerging technoscience of "transhuman-
ism" or "posthumanism" – creating bodies that are part
human and part machine, or even fully machine and activated
by the components of a human brain downloaded onto a com-
puter chip?[16] Or, perhaps even more controversially, as we
have just seen in relation to proposed research in the United

---

15 Habermas, *Future of Human Nature*, 25–37.
16 Brooks, *Flesh and Machines*.

States, what about the ethics of creating creatures that are part human, part animal?[17]

Surveys show that most Canadians and Americans are opposed to human "reproductive" cloning (making a child identical to an existing person) but fewer people oppose human "therapeutic" cloning (the creation of human embryos in order to use them as a source of stem cells for making therapeutic products).[18] But this only highlights our current moral confusion. Surely transmitting human life with the primary intention of killing the resulting embryos and doing so in order to make therapeutic products for the benefit of others – that is, commodifying embryos – does *not* fulfill the requirements of respect for the transmission of human life.

Respect for the Human Germ Cell Line

Yet another question we are the first humans to face: what does respect for the essence of human life, biologically speaking – the human germ cell line, the genes that are passed on from generation to generation – require of us? These genes are the product of 800 million years of evolution. We can now change that evolution in nanoseconds. What must we, may we, and must we not do? In changing an embryo's germ cell line,

---

17 Part mouse, to be specific; see N. Wade, "Stem Cell Mixing May Form a Human-Mouse Hybrid," *New York Times*, 27 November 2002. Even some scientists engaged in genetic research who are not usually regarded as conservative were strongly opposed to this on ethical grounds.

18 Ontario Consultants on Religious Tolerance, "Therapeutic Cloning: Ethics, Public Opinion, Legislation" (on-line, 16 April 2003, <www.religioustolerance.org/clo_ther1.htm>); Center for Genetics and Society, "Analysis: Public Opinion: Summary of Survey Results" (on-line, 16 April 2003, <www.genetics-and-society.org/analysis/opinion/summary.htm>).

we change not only that embryo but also all of its descendants
in like manner. Is it ever acceptable to do that?

Another way to ask the same question is: what does the
obligation to hold the human germ cell line in trust for future
generations, as the common heritage of humankind, require
of us? Does it mean, as many people believe, that we must
never intentionally change it, that alteration of the germ cell
line is never justified? What if we could eliminate a horrible
disease by changing just one gene and we knew it was reasonably safe to do that? Do we object to altering the human germ
cell line because we believe that it is inherently wrong to do
so, that no good purpose can ever be a justification for inter-
fering with it? Or do we believe that some interventions might
be justifiable – that it is not inherently wrong to intervene,
only that intervening is not presently justifiable because it is
too dangerous? Or do we fear that, once intervention is
allowed, no matter how much suffering we could eliminate
through it, we could not control the range of interventions
that would then occur and that many would be frivolous at
best, profoundly unacceptable at worst? (An extreme example
of the latter would be intentionally to disenhance the intelligence of certain embryos to create a class of people who
would be willing to work at the mundane, but necessary, tasks
that those whose intelligence had been genetically enhanced
would find too boring.)

It is important here to distinguish therapies that involve
genetic interventions on somatic cells from germ cell line interventions. Somatic cell genetic therapy only affects the genes of
that embryo (or, indeed, any person who is treated with it) not
the descendants of that embryo (or person). It can be justified
to treat serious disease, provided it has been shown to be reasonably safe and effective, which has not yet been established.
On the contrary, genetic therapies that have been used have
resulted in very harmful consequences, including death.[19]

19 Mike Bygrave, "False Dawns in Brave World of New Genetics," *The
Observer*, 22 December 2002 (on-line).

What about the justice issues raised by germ cell line alteration? Would only the rich have access to it, thus widening the
socio-economic gap? And what about the myriad of additional
ethical problems we would face because of the inevitable com-
mercialization of this technology? Speaking of commercial-
ization, is staking ownership claims on human genes – as
multinational pharmaceutical companies have done through
patents[20] – consistent with our fiduciary obligations in relation
to the human germ cell line? Almost certainly, it is not. Many
complex questions must be carefully analyzed if we are to act
ethically in this area.

On a broader scale, what are our obligations regarding
other living creatures' germ cell lines? May we just alter those
as suits us? At the very least, there should be a strong pre-
sumption against doing so; that is, a precautionary principle
should apply and those who wish to intervene should have a
very heavy burden of proof to show that what they propose is
fully justified.

RELIGIOUS VOICES IN THE PUBLIC SQUARE

In the past, we used a shared religion to find the shared principles and values on which we based our society, especially
those governing the two great events of each human life –
birth and death. That is not possible in multicultural, multire-
ligious secular democracies such as we have in North America.
But that does not mean that religious or spiritual beliefs
should now be excluded from our deliberations. On the contrary, they are an important element of a multivoiced public
discourse, and we are no more justified in excluding them
than we are in excluding views based on atheism or agnosticism. Moreover, the history of some of the most important
values in our secular society have their roots in a religious past,

---

20 Myriad Genetics, for example, in Salt Lake City, have patented
the human breast cancer genes BRAC1 and 2. See C. Abraham,
"Ontario to Fight for Gene Test," *Globe and Mail,* 7 January 2003.

just as our own experience of them may have roots in this or that religious present. To appreciate fully both the richness and the potential of these values they must not be artificially severed from that past or present, pursuant either to a false notion of neutrality or to an artificial political correctness.

A common image used to describe changes in values is that of a pendulum. Some see us as having swung away from values espoused in religion to a fully secular values base. That view is far too simplistic: the reality is much more complex and captured better in the image of a helix, like the DNA spiral with which we are now all so familiar. We have swung to secular values, but as we move forward and, consequently, back over some of our long-standing values, attitudes, beliefs, and traditions, we need to draw on the richness of knowledge, wisdom, and experience they encapsulate and incorporate that into the values that will guide us into the future.

That does not mean we will use religion directly as a basis for public policy. That is not acceptable in a secular society – one in which church and state are separate. But nowhere have we more to gain and less to lose in listening to the contribution that religions have to make than in charting a course through the unknown territory and unprecedented challenges raised by the new reprogenetic technoscience. Those challenges force us to grapple with the essence of human nature, human life, and human values – touching those very things that, over the aeons of human existence, we have used religion to mediate into our consciousness and to communicate about with each other.

CONCLUSION

It merits repeated notice that these unprecedented new challenges to respect for human life and, secondarily, to human dignity are being played out in relation to the youngest and, often, the oldest members of our community – genetics for the very young, euthanasia for the old. Perhaps that is no accident because we often test our principles, values, attitudes and beliefs at the margins, and here we are doing so at the two margins of life. In deciding what we must, may, and must not do, we should remember that the ethical tone of a society is set by how it treats its weakest, neediest, most vulnerable members, not how it treats those who are powerful, able, and can protect themselves. What ethical heritage will we hand on to our descendants? Our responses to the ethical issues raised by respect for human life, in the context of the new genetics and euthanasia, will play a major role in deciding that.

8

Taking Moral Difference Seriously
Morality after the Death of God

H. TRISTRAM ENGELHARDT, JR

THE MIRAGE OF MORAL CONSENSUS

The search for a first-order consensus is at best the pursuit of a mirage. The lack of consensus on issues bioethical spans the field of medicine from the beginning of human life, through health care allocation, to death. In contrast to a supposedly emerging secular "consensus," traditional Christians,[1] among others, oppose artificial insemination by donor, denounce pre-natal diagnosis and abortion, and hold physician-assisted suicide and euthanasia to be deeply morally misguided.[2] Confronted with such foundational disagreement, rather than

---

1 The term "traditional Christian" is used to identify those who endorse the moral commitments of the Christianity of the first millennium and the initial seven councils, which continues unaltered in Orthodox Christianity, forming the background for the development of the various Western Christian moralities.

2 The first- or second-century *Didache* states: "Thou shalt do no murder; thou shalt not commit adultery; thou shalt not commit sodomy; thou shalt not commit fornication; thou shalt not steal; thou shalt not use magic; thou shalt not use philtres; thou shalt not procure abortion, nor commit infanticide; thou shalt not covet thy neighbour's goods" (II, 2). See also Canon VII of the Canons of St Basil the Great: "Sodomists and bestialists and murderers and sorcerers and adulterers and idolaters deserve the same

searching for moral consensus it would be more honest and prudent to acknowledge the force and intractable character of moral diversity and then seek ways to collaborate in the face of moral difference. This can be done only if the depth of moral difference is acknowledged.

The difficulty is that moral diversity, much of which is religiously grounded, is obscured by two moral postulates that implicitly undergird the current dominant secular culture: (1) the agnostic postulate that invites all to act and speak as if God did not exist and (2) the ecumenical religious postulate that invites all to pray and act as if wrong religious choices will not lead to eternally adverse outcomes. Religiously grounded moral difference is discounted because of the demand that we act as if God did not exist and as if religion lacked moral and metaphysical truth value. This contemporary moral ethos has its roots in three transformative cultural developments: (1) the moralization of religion, (2) the cultural reduction of theology, and (3) the cosmic deorientation of existence and history. The resultant moral ethos discounts the significance of religious morality and, in particular, traditional Christian morality, which locates moral claims within a context of transcendent commitments. These commitments, because they are grounded in transcendent claims, exacerbate the first-order moral controversies at the heart of morality.

The cleft between immanently and transcendentally grounded morality is a source of the irresolvability, through sound rational argument, of many bioethical debates. The

---

condemnation, so that whatever rule you have as regarding the others observe it also in regard to these persons" (Sts Nicodemus and Agapius, eds., *The Rudder of the Orthodox Catholic Church* [New York: Luna Printing, 1983], 793). As to physician-assisted suicide, early Christianity took for granted that suicide, hence also aiding or abetting suicide, was forbidden. See, for example, the answer to Question xiv in "The 18 Canons of Timothy, the Most Holy Archbishop of Alexandria" (*The Rudder*, 898).

conflicting positions are grounded in different foundational premises and rules of moral evidence. Not only is consensus in this circumstance a mirage, but the denial of moral difference can be offensive to those who wish to affirm it. It is plausible that in some cases the very attempt to discount and deny moral diversity can itself provoke a violent affirmation of moral difference. In our fallen moral state we are best advised to pursue means to live peaceably in the presence of substantive moral diversity rather than to seek a first-order moral consensus. Our consensus should be that we have no first-order moral consensus regarding a wide range of important moral issues. The challenge is to live peaceably with foundational moral disagreement.

BEYOND THE POLIS: SOCIETY AS A PLACE FOR MORALLY DIVERSE, PEACEABLE COMMUNITIES

Aristotle casts a dark shadow of unwarranted expectations across contemporary understandings of political structure. He invites us to consider society as one community built around a single moral vision or consensus. In this account, society and community collapse into each other. All is to be organized in the hope that society can be directed by a common moral and cultural understanding, which Aristotle holds requisite for judging and distributing offices according to merit. Towards the goal of sustaining such a polity, he envisages the ideal city-state nurtured by a common view of *paedeia* compassing not more than 100,000 free men.[3] It is a polity inhospitable to foreigners and resident aliens. As he puts it in the *Politics*: "But if the citizens of a state are to judge and to distribute offices according to merit, then they must know each other's characters; where they do not possess this knowledge, both the election to offices and the decision of lawsuits will go wrong. When the population is very large they are manifestly settled

---

3 *Nicomachean Ethics*, IX.10l30,1171a.

at haphazard, which clearly ought not to be. Besides, in an over-populous state foreigners and resident aliens will readily acquire the rights of citizens, for who will find them out?"[4] Aristotle may correctly diagnose some of the ills of large-scale societies. However, his prescription for their treatment is, to say the very least, inapplicable to contemporary life in large-scale societies and multicultural states. The populations of contemporary states are two to three magnitudes greater than that of Greek city-states. Also, there tend to be numerous foreigners and resident aliens, and no shared view of the common good.

Aristotle offers this picture of the ideal polity, even though he served as tutor to Alexander the Great, who forged Greece's first multicultural, multiethnic political structures. The distant heirs of the Alexandrian invasions produced a Hellenic culture that, among other things, provoked successful armed rebellion by Judas Maccabeus in 165 BC, leading to the rededication of the Temple, celebrated in the feast of Hanukkah. This armed uprising was directed against the aspirant humanist consensus of the regime of Antiochus Epiphanes, who had desecrated the Temple in 168 BC and who attempted, among other things, to bring his Jewish subjects to abandon their traditional laws and customs in order to forge them with others into one people united in a Hellenic moral consensus.[5] Antiochus also sought to extirpate a form of religious belief that, to Hellenic moral sensibilities, was fanatically at odds with the prevailing morality. This included an attempt to prohibit what, for the Greek consciousness, was child abuse in the form of Jewish male circumcision.[6] Contemporary

---

4 *Politics*, VII.1326b12–22.

5 Grabbe, *Judaism from Cyrus to Hadrian*, 1:281–5.

6 Hellenized inhabitants of the Levant ridiculed Jews for being circumcised, a state that became evident when Jewish youth exercised naked in Greek gymnasia. In general there was a revulsion towards circumcision, and cosmetic operations were introduced to reverse its effects (see E. Wallerstein, "Circumcision: Ritual

reflections on the possibilities for common collaboration and agreement occur in a circumstance much closer to that of Alexander's empire than to Aristotle's city-state. We compass a true diversity of moral visions.

After 11 September 2001 human moral diversity should be more apparent than ever: people are deeply divided concerning the common good, the dignity of humans, the equality of persons, and the significance of human rights. There are foundational and strident moral disputes as to whether abortionists are murderers or people who liberate women from the tyranny of biological forces and traditional patriarchal social structures. There are similar disagreements as to whether those who assist in suicide are collaborators in self-murder or people who liberate others from unnecessary suffering, who defend human freedom against blind natural forces. Members of many traditional religious communities have moral and metaphysical grounds for a wide range of what are now considered to be provocative moral positions, including condemning sexual intercourse outside of the marriage of a man and a woman. They may recognize men and women as equals who are nevertheless ordered according to hierarchical gender-specific roles, such as the male priesthood and episcopate of Roman Catholicism and Orthodox Christianity. Traditional Christian views of sexual relations, early human life, gender roles, the significance of suffering, and the proper ending of life are deeply at odds with those normatively affirmed in the dominant intellectual culture of posttraditional, liberal-

---

Surgery or Surgical Ritual?" *Medicine and Law* 2 [1983]: 88). Lamentably, there are again movements to prohibit male circumcision when undertaken for ritual purposes, bolstered by the view that circumcision should be understood as a form of criminal assault. For a study of some of the issues, see Gregory Boyle, J. Steven Svoboda, Christian Price, and J. Neville Turner, "Circumcision of Healthy Boys: Criminal Assault?" *Journal of Law and Medicine* 7 (February 2000): 301–10.

cosmopolitan societies. These disagreements are blocks against substantive consensus.[7]

They are also matters about which individuals and communities are emotionally divided – elements of the human drama that define the character of our relations with each other as well as the battles of the culture wars.[8] In so far as one holds that such disagreement is real and not likely to abate, one has good grounds not to pursue consensus but, instead, to pursue the articulation of political structures that allow a polity peaceably to encompass real moral and religious pluralism. Aspirations to consensus envisage political outcomes in terms of zero-sum games. Either one's own community's view of moral flourishing wins the game and is established as the regnant moral vision to the detriment of other views, or it loses. Instead of directing ourselves to the goal of a consensus universally imposed through the coercive force of law, we should envisage policy approaches that can compass a plurality of peaceable moral visions, allowing uncoerced collaboration in the face of real moral diversity. For example, we might envisage legislation allowing physicians opposed to abortion, after making a summary declaration of their moral commitments, to be free of any obligation in administrative or tort law to refer patients to physicians who provide pre-natal diagnosis

---

7 Absent a canonical experience of God or of the truth, humans are left to the expedient of drawing authority for common actions from themselves. In that such a moral account provides no substantive understanding of virtue or of flourishing, the necessary side constraints on moral deportment under these circumstances (e.g., the agreement of the collaborating persons) can be transformed by a hunger for moral substance into guiding moral goods. The result is an affirmation of the value of self-determination, expressed in an endorsement of empty mutual affirmation (not mere toleration) of each person's choices, as central to the dominant socio-democratic ethos. See further Engelhardt, *Foundations of Christian Bioethics*, 137–48.

8 For an introduction to the latter, see Hunter, *Culture Wars*.

and abortion. At a constitutional level, we would need to recover the important relationship between moral diversity and limited democracy.

Constitutional limited democracy is a political solution to governance in the face of moral diversity and disagreement. Limited democracy with robust rights to free speech is fashioned as a response to moral diversity and in order to protect minority moral visions from the tyranny of the majority.[9] The structure of limited democracies presupposes that there are important political goods to be achieved within a state that does not conceive of its society as equivalent to a moral community but, instead, focuses on collaboration in the face of real moral disagreement. Rather than the guiding image being that of the Aristotelian *polis*, in a constitutional limited democracy it is that of a civil society that constitutes a framework within which communities and individuals can peaceably and substantively disagree regarding matters of utmost importance.[10] In this circumstance, (1) the state need not invest energies in discounting and marginalizing moral difference, (2) divergent moral communities need not defend their moral integrity against a hostile state, (3) citizens can gain the civil skill of living with robust moral difference, and (4) the liberty and integrity of personal and communal moral commitments can be affirmed.

9 Beset by numerous accounts of moral rationality, by default secular polities are constrained to draw authority from the consent of their citizens. As a consequence, such polities cannot provide authorization for more than what can be created within the constraints of a constitutional limited democracy. This is much less than that to which a social-democratic polity aspires. See Engelhardt, *Foundations of Bioethics*, 2nd ed., chaps 3 and 4.

10 Put positively: rather than understanding society as a community, we should seek a social space wherein numerous moral communities may peaceably collaborate. Under this model, religiously based hospital systems, for example, would be free of any obligation to provide (or refer for) treatment regarded as morally inappropriate, while continuing to function within a diversified heath care network.

It may be added that robust guarantees of free speech protect the notion of tolerance from being corrupted into forced acceptance of the views of a dominant moral community, even if only by coerced silence. Traditionally, tolerance requires eschewing force rather than eschewing public statements regarding the morally or metaphysically ill-directed character of another person's or community's religion, moral views, or way of life. In the absence of such frank discourse, it is difficult to articulate publicly that choices of religion, lifestyle, and morality are as serious as are choices of medical treatments (or indeed that the former may in some cases involve substantial risks of spiritual harm). When the public rendering of adverse judgments regarding the consequences of such choices is discouraged as a form of hate speech, then a particular moral vision is enshrined that is at odds with the commitments of those who embrace traditional moral-metaphysical visions. It is an irony that diversity is often affirmed primarily in terms of skin pigmentation, race, language, and morally unfreighted customs rather than in terms of the real moral differences that separate individuals and communities. Imposed public silence on such issues impoverishes moral discourse by obscuring the seriousness of the choices at stake.

MORAL DIFFERENCES ARE REAL AND PERSISTENT

Alasdair MacIntyre aptly observes that there are two striking characteristics of contemporary moral and public policy debates. Regarding issues of central moral concern, not only are the debates interminable but there is no apparent common basis by which they can be resolved through sound rational argument.[11] Kant attempted to avoid this state of

---

11 See MacIntyre, *After Virtue*, 6: "The most striking feature of contemporary moral utterance is that so much of it is used to express disagreements; and the most striking feature of the debates in which these disagreements are expressed is their interminable

affairs by equating morality with rationality, by deriving moral authority from rationality, and by claiming all to be members, witting or no, of a universal kingdom of ends (albeit one that looks suspiciously like a secularized version of Kant's own pietistic Protestant morality). The Kantian Enlightenment dream of discovering that we are all united, despite our differences, in one moral rationality and, therefore, in one community appears to be blocked by the stubborn fact that we do not share one moral rationality.

Consider, for example, a difference between Orthodox Christianity and Roman Catholicism. The first understands theology, moral or otherwise, to be primarily noetic – that is, "mystical" – with the result that at least half of the great Orthodox theologians of the twentieth century never completed a university education,[12] while the second understands theology principally as an academic or scholarly undertaking. In this spirit, the Roman Catholic Congregation for the Doctrine of the Faith can opine that "through the course of centuries, theology has progressively developed into a true and proper science."[13] These two religions, even though related, do not share a common understanding of moral and theological epistemology, much less a common understanding of exemplary knowers. However, for the establishment of a consensus through sound rational argument, the participants in a controversy need to be in agreement regarding fundamental moral premises and rules of moral evidence. Yet this is exactly

---

character. I do not mean by this just that such debates go on and on and on – although they do – but also that they apparently can find no terminus. There seems to be no rational way of securing moral agreement in our culture."

12 As Evagrios the Solitary put it in the fourth century: "If you are a theologian, you will pray truly. And if you pray truly, you are a theologian" ("On Prayer," *Philokalia*, 1:62). See also Vlachos, *Mind of the Orthodox Church.*

13 "Instruction on the Ecclesial Vocation of the Theologian," *Origins* 20 (5 July 1990): 120.

what is not the case and what is at issue. The disagreements concern basic principles and rules of inference.

This is also the case for secular moral controversies. For example, divergent premises define the disputes regarding the moral preferability of American or German two-tier approaches to health care allocation over Canadian health care policy (the latter effectively prohibiting the purchase of better basic health care). Comparative assessments depend, inter alia, on the ranking of such fundamental human goods as liberty, equality, prosperity, and security. Even if we some-how agree that this is the correct short list of social-moral desiderata, we are still not able to determine which approach to health care policy has the better consequences – unless we already know how to rank these basic goods or goals. We cannot agree about such a ranking unless we already share a background theory, account, narrative, or vision of the good. Appeals to preferences will not succeed either, unless we are already in agreement as to how to correct preferences, to com-pare impassioned versus rationally considered preferences, to discount the satisfaction of preferences over time, and so on. Nor will it do to appeal to the decisions of disinterested observers or hypothetical contractors or decision makers. They will not choose in any particular way unless they are fitted with a particular moral sense. Again, this is what is at issue: which moral vision should guide? In addition, if one recognizes the existence of fundamentally different views regarding the authority of the state and of the trumping authority of private choice and property, then matters become even more difficult. Individuals argue out of divergent moral- and political-theoretical perspectives.

When these differences are enhanced by differences grounded in metaphysical and, especially, religious commit-ments, as with respect to the moral probity of abortion, clon-ing, artificial insemination from donors, sexual relations outside the marriage of a man and a woman, physician-assisted suicide, and euthanasia, then any expectation of a resolution of such debates through sound rational argument is even more comprehensibly blocked. The parties are separated by different understandings of the deep nature of being and the character of moral knowledge, not to mention different rankings of values. To resolve such controversies, one must grant at the outset a particular characterization of what is at stake in the dispute and of how it can, in principle, be settled. Which is to say, in the face of foundational moral and metaphysical differences, claims to closure by sound rational argument will at best involve begging the question, arguing in a circle, or engaging in an infinite regress.[14]

All of this is to repeat what should be apparent: moral difference is fundamental and persistent. This is not to deny that there are various fads in the history of thought and morality, with the result that those who live within particular moral communities in particular eras may find it difficult even to imagine that others could reject the premises that they find self-evidently framing their consensus. As a consequence, when members of such communities confront the moral differences defining the battles in their culture wars, they may discount them. Such discounting usually presumes that the other will come to accept the judging party's basic premises and rules of inference because they appear to those who affirm them to be self-evident. Conversions of moral, epistemological, and metaphysical commitments do occur. However, they cannot be guaranteed as the basis of a consensus. Most important, they cannot be delivered through sound rational argument. Hence the intractability of moral difference.

CONSENSUS AND ITS AMBIGUITIES

It is important to recognize the numerous meanings, if not the strategic ambiguity, of the term "consensus."[15] Four meanings deserve note, especially the last:

---

14 See Engelhardt, Jr, and Caplan, eds., *Scientific Controversies.*

15 See further Engelhardt, "Consensus Formation: The Creation of an Ideology," *Cambridge Quarterly* 11 (Winter 2002): 7–16. See also Bayertz, *Concept of Moral Consensus.*

1 *Consensus as unanimous consent*
This is the etymological sense of consensus: being of one spirit or feeling about an issue.[16] Such complete agreement, although theoretically possible in some communities and specially structured religious bodies, is impossible in contemporary large-scale societies.

2 *Consensus as a mark of truth*
Consensus as widespread agreement may be a mark of truth under certain circumstances. But it is neither a sufficient condition nor, from the perspective of the history of science, an especially promising one.

3 *Consensus as an authorizing majority*
Here consensus is not consensus *sensu stricto* but, rather, the requirement of a supermajority as part of a voting procedure or principle of governance in order (a) to protect against rapid, dramatic ideological swings, (b) to guarantee that the initial rights of participants in a polity will not be easily abrogated by a new majority, and/or (c) to provide the mass coercion needed for a Realpolitik that seeks to guarantee sufficient support for the enforceability of substantive policies.

4 *Consensus as a rhetorical device or ideology*
As a rhetorical ploy, consensus can be invoked against minority views so as to label them extremist, controversial, non-mainstream, or irrational, thereby threatening minority stakeholders with being marginalized if not subjected to the coercive constraint of the ruling majority (e.g., the voicing of minority moral opinions being forbidden under the rubric of hate speech, leading to formal or informal barriers against advancing substantive moral judgments). In this fashion, the dominant moral community can employ appeals to consensus to enlarge its hegemony by creating rules at law and public policy to enforce politically and

---

16 "Consensus: unanimity or general agreement in matters of opinion, evidence, testimony, etc." *Webster's New International Dictionary*, 2nd ed. (Springfield: Merriam, 1960), 567.

morally correct discourse and behavior (e.g., sanctioning as unacceptable a physician's refusal on moral and religious grounds to prescribe Viagra for an unmarried man or a homosexual).

This last use of consensus is disingenuous and morally inappropriate to limited democratic polities. It collides with the very pluralism that characterizes large-scale democracies. Moral difference is not only real and persistent but, when peaceable, defines life within a limited democracy.

The plausibility of consensus is nevertheless fortified by the ways in which committees and commissions generally function when developing public policy. Such committees rarely come to a consensus even in the third sense; rather, the usual dynamics of public policy are such that they favour the creation of bodies able to declare the establishment of a favoured "consensus" in the fourth sense.[17] In this fashion, such committees serve to discount, dampen, and marginalize moral disagreement. If a government created a commission composed of persons of truly diverse moral commitments, then the debates would be as interminable as are those in society at large. Consider what would occur if one appointed a monk from Mount Athos, an Orthodox Jewish rabbi, a traditional Muslim, a feminist, an atheist, a socialist, and a libertarian to a panel to determine the content of a sex-education curriculum for public and private schools in the Province of Quebec. The debate would be sustained but without hope of conclusion. There would be disagreements regarding not only the advisability of such instruction (not to mention its content) but also the legitimacy of public education itself (as well as the authority of the state to mandate the content of education in private schools). Out of a recognition of this circumstance, as

---

17 The result of reflections by commissions on proper deportment can be the creation of an official morality for public governance. See, for example, National Commission for the Protection of Human Subjects of Biomedical and Behavioral Research, *The Belmont Report*.

well as from a desire to establish a particular policy, politicians are often tempted to appoint people with moral commitments similar to their own. This is so that those appointed can then discover that they are able to reconstruct their commitments in a common moral language, leading to a common and "appropriate" set of recommendations. Those appointed need not share identical theoretical views of the nature of morality; it is enough that they share the same background moral vision. This modus operandi tends to obscure moral disagreement, including the foundational ambiguities in the concept of consensus itself. This also serves to delegitimize nonconforming moral viewpoints.

These tendencies were reinforced early in the development of bioethics by the influential role of Beauchamp and Childress's *Principles of Biomedical Ethics* (1979). These two bioethicists began their reflections from similar political and moral commitments. They discovered that they could produce and employ common, middle-level moral principles despite the circumstance that one was a rule-utilitarian and the other a deontologist. From this success many wrongly concluded that all persons share one common morality and therefore (implicitly) one common bioethics. They did not appreciate that these bioethicists had simply reconstructed from two different theoretical frameworks the common morality of the two authors, who were then able to collaborate effectively in using their four middle-level principles (i.e., autonomy, beneficence, non-maleficence, and justice). They did not acknowledge that, although moralities may share common concerns regarding lying, taking property, and killing other humans (not to mention liberty, equality, prosperity, and security), moralities are distinguished by their settled judgments regarding when lying, taking property, and killing humans are good, bad, or indifferent (not to mention how one ranks primary moral goods). It is the constellation of such settled judgments that sustains a particular morality. For those who do *not* share such a common morality, the use of middle-level principles (e.g., such as an appeal to the importance of autonomy, beneficence, non-maleficence, and justice) will not disclose agreement. For instance, imagine a traditional

Christian and a liberal cosmopolitan atheist both invoking the principle of beneficence with regard to abortion. They will only appreciate better, at both theoretical and practical levels, the depth of their disagreements.

MORAL DIFFERENCES
AFTER THE DEATH OF GOD

The socio-democratic ethos dominant in contemporary Western polities systematically discounts moral difference by resituating metaphysically anchored transcendent moral claims within the horizon of the finite and the immanent. This is accomplished by recasting moral concerns in terms of the following two practical postulates:

1 *The agnostic moral postulate*
   In public, one acts and speaks as if there were no God and, therefore, as if one were confronting the task of making sense of human life within an ultimately senseless universe. As a result, a bioethics articulated within this context must be directed to goods appreciable within the horizon of the finite and the immanent. This circumstance tends to place the accent on procedural mechanisms for resolving disputes.
2 *The ecumenical religious postulate*
   If, despite the agnostic postulate, one does engage in public religious discourse or prayer, such discourse or prayer must be free of claims regarding transcendent truth. That is, one must act and speak as if religious concerns did not involve matters of fact, as if religion (unlike, say, medical interventions) were not a matter regarding which one can be right or wrong.[18]

---

18 Ecumenism notwithstanding, religions differ with respect to Who exactly God is and of how appropriately to turn to Him; that is, they are separated by their accounts of right worship, right belief, and its importance.

These postulates can be better appreciated against the background of three significant cultural developments that occurred over the last two and one-quarter centuries – developments that mark the emergence of an ethos within which moral difference is poorly appreciated:

1 *The moralization of religion*
In great measure Immanuel Kant effected the third Protestant Reformation when he attempted to articulate the public truth value of Christianity in terms of its moral implications. The force of this position is that religion is interpreted as concerned with the good, not with the holy.[19] In consequence it should not matter to which religion one belongs so long as one lives a life committed to the pursuit of the good (i.e., the immanently good, including social justice).

2 *The cultural reduction of theology*
Hegel recognized that one outcome of the Enlightenment is that the substance of theology has been philosophically recast: theology's higher truth is construed as its cultural or intellectual significance. As Emil Fackenheim perceptively notes, for Hegel the Christian God is "the last of all gods who exhausts all religious possibilities … [h]ence this last God points to a radically post-religious future, and the bourgeois, Protestant human freedom already actual points to a radically secular freedom which is yet to become actual."[20] This view has indeed led to a thoroughly secularized public

---

19 Traditional Christianity locates the pursuit of justice and the pursuit of the good within the context of the pursuit of holiness (i.e., true righteousness). It recognizes the moral life as focused first and foremost on discharging the first great commandment (Matt. 22:37ff.), to love God with all one's heart, soul, and mind. It recognizes that one can rightly discharge the second commandment – to love one's neighbour as oneself – only in the light of the first. One can only love one's neighbour rightly if one loves and worships God rightly.

20 Fackenheim, *Religious Dimension in Hegel's Thought,* 239.

Christianity, which attempts to set aside the transcendent claims of faith by relocating them as cultural images aimed at self-fulfillment and self-realization.

3 *The cosmic de-orientation of existence and history*

After the death of God, it is no longer possible in the dominant culture to discern an ultimate purpose and direction in human and cosmic history. In such a context, morality (including bioethics) cannot determine a canonical or normative goal for the direction of human evolution. In a cosmos that appears to come from nowhere and to be to no ultimate purpose, there are numerous different and always limited accounts of the meaning of human presence and evolution, which must in the end be recognized as more or less arbitrary alternatives.

In consequence of these developments all moral (and bioethical) questions and answers are placed fully within the horizon of the finite and the immanent, as are concerns with human dignity and human rights. Human dignity is no longer grounded in a status conveyed by God to humans, through creation in his image and (on the Christian account) through the incarnation, which gives humans the opportunity to become gods by grace.[21] Human dignity can no longer be acknowledged as anchored in a reality independent of human concerns; that is, in the Creator and in the deep nature of created being. It is lodged instead in the achievement of certain goods, or the honouring of certain constraints on human choice, integral to particular accounts of what it means to hold oneself praiseworthy or blameworthy. In such circumstances the task is to designate an immanent surrogate for the divine and so to ground, as best one can, claims regarding human dignity and human rights. In the Enlightenment, reason was invoked to serve as such a surrogate. However, the status of claims regarding morality does not remain the same

---

21 In Athanasius' famous words, "He was made man that we might be made god[s]" (*On the Incarnation*, 54.3).

when reason is substituted for Christianity's transcendent, omnipotent, personal God, Who can impose ultimate sanctions for immoral action. Absent God, the seriousness of morality is radically discounted. In Elizabeth Anscombe's words, "it is as if the notion 'criminal' were to remain when criminal law and criminal courts had been abolished and forgotten."[22] *Nulla lex sine poena* applies to the moral law as well.

Kant himself realized this. In response, he invoked an "as if" existence of God and immortality, thus, in a backhanded fashion, guaranteeing a unity of the good, a harmony of the right and the good, and a coordination of the justification and motivation of the moral life.[23] Not surprisingly, this solution showed little durability, so that all too human accounts are all we have left. As Richard Rorty observes, "we can keep the notion of 'morality' just insofar as we can cease to think of morality as the voice of the divine part of ourselves."[24]

---

22 G.E.M. Anscombe, "Modern Moral Philosophy," *Philosophy* 33 (January 1958): 6. Indeed, as Anscombe argues: "The concepts of obligation, and duty – moral obligation and moral duty, that is to say – and of what is morally right and wrong, and of the moral sense of 'ought,' ought to be jettisoned if this is psychologically possible, because they are survivals, or derivatives from survivals, from an earlier conception of ethics which no longer generally survives, and are only harmful without it" (1).

23 "Morality, by itself, constitutes a system. Happiness, however, does not do so, save in so far as it is distributed in exact proportion to morality. But this is possible only in the intelligible world, under a wise Author and Ruler. Such a Ruler, together with life in such a world, which we must regard as a future world, reason finds itself constrained to assume; otherwise it would have to regard the moral laws as empty figments of the brain, since without this postulate the necessary consequence which it itself connects with these laws could not follow." See Kant, *Critique of Pure Reason*, 639, A811=B839. His "as if" language is of the First Critique.

24 Rorty, *Contingency, Irony, and Solidarity*, 59.

A metaphysical and moral chasm thus opens between those whose point of reference is a transcendent personal Creator and those who regard all of existence as ultimately purposeless. If the universe inexplicably arises out of a naked singularity, and if human nature is merely the result of random mutations, selective pressure, genetic drift, cosmic catastrophes, and the constraints of chemical and physical laws, then human nature and human life are a surd. As Gianni Vattimo appreciates, this state of affairs is at the root of our profound cultural rupture: "the death of God, which is at once the culmination and conclusion of metaphysics, is also the crisis of humanism."[25] The *humanum* of humanism's focus becomes a blind outcome of contingent processes, depriving it of any metaphysical gravitas. At the same time morality must be recognized as rooted in human narratives, which are multiple. Reason, which was to serve as a secular surrogate for the Christian God, fractures into a polytheism of rationalities, yielding the intractable pluralism of postmodernity. Moral pluralism ceases to be a mere fact of the matter and becomes a defining characteristic of the secular moral predicament. Atheism, observes Vattimo, appears "as another catastrophic Tower of Babel."[26]

After the cultural death of God, and in the context of a seemingly senseless universe, claims of human dignity, equality, and respect have no depth beyond that of the particular accounts of the project of human morality in which they are anchored. These multiple narratives define the human condition in such a way that one is faced with competing moralities and accounts of morality, among which a choice cannot be made in a principled fashion on the basis of sound rational

---

25 Vattimo, *End of Modernity*, 33.
26 Ibid. 31.

argument.[27] This state of affairs is itself taken to be normative, such that the moral and political space that results is inhospitable to any content-rich or comprehensive moral view that challenges this polytheism of moral viewpoints. In this context meaning is sought in a liberal cosmopolitan commitment to (1) interpersonal moral affirmation, (2) the pursuit of self-fulfillment, and (3) the realization of self-satisfaction understood in terms of concerns nested fully within the horizon of the immanent and the finite. Within these constraints a pluralism of stories, a multiplicity of accounts, can be affirmed.

The traditional Christian response to this state of affairs involves not an appeal to sound rational argument (which can only further mediate the content available within the domain of the immanent and finite) but, rather, to an invitation to the noetic experience of Truth as a radically transcendent Who.[28] The determined secularist must dismiss this response from the field of public discourse because the invitation to a noetically available transcendent can show the way beyond the horizon of the immanent. From the secularist's perspective, the way out of the impasse of postmodernity through an experience

---

27 Given the inability to support by sound rational argument a principled choice among competing accounts of human morality, the project of secular morality is framed by an unavoidable epistemological skepticism (but not necessarily a moral metaphysical skepticism) grounded in a systematic moral indeterminacy (which need not lead to a moral relativism).

28 Sakharov, *We Shall See Him as He Is*, stresses that "without real experience of God or cosmic spiritual phenomena, possession of intellectual information does not reveal the meaning of religion – does not lead to experimental knowledge of Primal Being – of God, that is. By 'knowledge' I mean ingress into the very Act of Eternity. 'This is life eternal, that they might know thee, the only true God' [John 17:3]" (8). "Our way to knowledge of God lies not through books but through faith in Christ's word. This faith brings our mind down into the heart, consumed by the flame of love for Christ" (87).

of the divine is unacceptable. Such a resolution would sanctify and therefore transform the immanent, setting aside postmodernity through a confrontation with Truth. Claims of a transcendent God will therefore be appreciated as lying at the root of non-negotiable, and in this sense fundamentalist, religious commitments. Since the dominant secular ethos can engage no explicit transcendent claims, nor support views of human relations not articulable within the horizon of immanence and finitude (a point made by John Rawls),[29] it must oppose their entry into the public forum. Claims will be regarded as unacceptably fundamentalist if, among other things, they assert that transcendent considerations can in some circumstances trump those of the secular social-democratic ethos.

LIVING WITH REAL MORAL DIFFERENCE

Moral difference is real. Moral difference is compounded by metaphysical difference. It is not simply that humans are divided by different rankings of values or, indeed, commitments to different values. Humans are divided by radically different accounts of the meaning of human life and of the universe. In the ruins of post-Christian societies such as those of the West, persons and communities are separated by fundamentally different appreciations of the human enterprise and of the significance of reality. Those who do not embrace the agnostic moral postulate and the ecumenical religious postulate will resist the moralization of religion and the cultural reduction of theology. As a consequence, such persons and their communities will live in a life-world structured by a divergent orientation to ultimate meaning and purpose.

Such is not the case for the emerging secular culture. Within that culture there is a paradoxical disparity between power and moral-metaphysical insight, so that humans find

---

29 John Rawls, "The Idea of Public Reason Revisited," *University of Chicago Law Review* 64 (Summer 1997): 765–807.

themselves with more power over themselves and their environment than ever before but with less of an understanding of how (or how much of) this power should be used. For example, there is a residual sense that profound issues are at stake regarding human reproductive cloning and the fact that humans now have the ability to direct human evolution. Absent a point of ultimate orientation, however, no particular account of direction or purpose can succeed in being canonical. Within the horizon of the immanent, accounts of the ultimate significance of human and cosmic history collapse into a polytheism of alternative narratives, each with its own hermeneutic circle, none of which is anchored in the depths of Being. One has at best alternative stories, with the result that humans are lost in their stories, in their texts, isolated from any final purpose. As Walker Percy aptly observed, they find themselves lost in the cosmos.[30]

The intractable moral pluralism that results engenders more than conflicting appreciations of the human good and of human flourishing, immanently construed. What is most striking is the gulf that opens up between those who recognize ultimate meaning and those who attempt to make do within the horizon of the immanent. The field of bioethics is a testimony to this gulf.[31] Bioethics came into existence in the United

---

30 Percy, *Lost in the Cosmos*.

31 The term "bioethics" appears to have been coined by Van Rensselaer Potter; see "Bioethics, the Science of Survival," *Perspectives in Biology and Medicine* 14 (1970): 127–53; "Biocybernetics and Survival," *Zygon* 5 (1970): 229–46; and *Bioethics: Bridge to the Future* (Englewood Cliffs: Prentice-Hall, 1971). Potter conceived of bioethics as an environmentally friendly ethos and lifestyle. See Potter, *Global Bioethics*. The term was either independently coined or recast in its meaning by Sargent Shriver and/or André Hellegers (Sargent Shriver, letter to author, 26 January 2001). For an overview of the development of bioethics, see Jonsen, *Birth of Bioethics*; see also Warren Reich, "The Word 'Bioethics': Its Birth and the Legacies of Those Who Shaped Its Meaning," *Kennedy Institute of Ethics Journal* 4 (1994): 319–36.

States in the 1970s to fill a moral vacuum created by the secularization of American society,[32] the deprofessionalization of medicine from a guild to a trade,[33] and the deconstruction of traditional authority figures.[34]

Bioethicists and clinical bioethics consultants were to become the secular theologians and chaplains of the new era. Their attempt to bring a guiding ethos to health care, however, has run aground on the shoals of moral pluralism, from which there appears to be no escape through discursive moral rationality without begging the question, arguing in a circle, or engaging an infinite regress. Bioethicists and clinical bioethics consultants have had to step back from all claims of metaphysical depth. The result has been a banalization of human sexuality, reproduction, suffering, dying, and death, without any remedy available within the horizon of immanence where these bioethicists and consultants ply their trade. For example, confronted by death, they can at best tell patients about their rights to control their treatment and to end their lives, but they cannot tell them what life, suffering, and death are about. They may even tell them about stories they might find comforting. But truth and meaning are beyond their compass.

There is not only moral pluralism, but a profound moral rupture in contemporary moral discourse. This rupture separates traditional Christians, Jews, Muslims, and others who

---

32 Compare, for example, *United States v. Macintosh*, 283 US 605 (1931) and *Tessim Zorach v. Andrew G. Clauson et al.*, 343 US 306, 96 L ed 954, 72 S Ct 679 (1951).

33 See *The United States of America, Appellants, v. The American Medical Association, A Corporation: The Medical Society of the District of Columbia, A Corporation, et al.*, 317 US 519 (1943); and *American Medical Assoc. v. Federal Trade Comm'n*, 638F.2d 443 (2d Cir. 1980).

34 The criticism of traditional authority figures had important expressions in critiques of medical paternalism, leading to the establishment of the "reasonable and prudent" standard for disclosure in informed consent for treatment. See *Canterbury v. Spence*, 464 f.2d 772 (DC Cir. 1972).

recognize that the universe has deep meaning and purpose from those who prefer to act as if there were no God and as if religious differences were merely matters of culture rather than matters of truth. The attempt to moralize religion, culturally reduce theology, and disengage existence and history from ultimate orientation has served only to bring into more stark contrast the conflict between cultures, particularly between the dominant agnostic culture and traditional religious cultures. These conflicts will define the character of moral discourse for the foreseeable future. In this circumstance, rather than pursuing a vain hope of consensus, we would do better to invest our energies in the articulation of political structures and procedures that can peaceably encompass substantial metaphysical and moral diversity without seeking either to discount it or to marginalize it.

9

Of Secularity and Civil Religion

DOUGLAS FARROW

In *Beyond Idols* Princeton sociologist of religion Richard Fenn offers a vision of secular society as a society characterized above all by its resolute openness. Such a society – which has never yet existed but is promisingly hinted at in Canada, for example – is devoted to the immanent rather than the transcendent, to the temporal rather than the eternal, indeed to the temporary rather than the permanent. It is not a society that rejects the Sacred but only the sacred. That is, it understands the Sacred as "pure potential" and rejects any attempt to fix it, to manage it, to close it off, to institutionalize it, and so to serve it with unnecessary suffering through the sacrificial maintenance of sacred myths or mysteries. A truly secular society is a society that dares to live without the idols of patriotism, civil religion, or creeds of any kind: "For a society to exist more fully in time, to be more secular, it is necessary for the living to be free of appeals to sacred memory and eschatological hope. Rather than revere a continuing and fixed deposit of memory and tradition, a secular society turns its memories and traditions over to a continuing and democratic discourse about the past in relation to the present. Such a discourse is necessary if that society is to enjoy realistic degrees of freedom ... In a secular society one is continually exposed to the passage of time without the comforting illusions of transcendence."[1]

That Fenn should look to Canada as a sign of hope for the continued advance of secularity will not surprise anyone. It is not just that Canadians are not so given as are their American cousins to displays of religiosity, civil or otherwise. Some Canadians, at least, have learned to pride themselves on the notion that "the Canadian experience" is precisely that of a perpetual experiment.[2] Nor will it surprise that Fenn (being a disciple of Bryan Wilson) should identify Protestant Christianity, which is by nature iconoclastic, as the major source of the secularizing drive, though this might make some Canadians – not only his fellow Protestants but those who have laboured hard to remove Christianity of any kind from its public pedestal – uncomfortable.[3] But Canadian or not, Protestant or not, we should share the Reverend Fenn's concern to develop a form of secularity that eschews idolatry. For idols are oppressive. They rob us of our freedom, beginning with our religious freedom.[4]

---

1 Fenn, *Beyond Idols*, 7. Fenn's curious blend of Kantian, Hegelian, and Nietzschean ideas with Christianity has a precedent in Thomas Altizer, for whom pure openness also takes the place of God. (Compare Farrow, *Ascension and Ecclesia*, 26of.) However, the incoherence of Fenn's treatment of transcendence and immanence, or of temporality, must not detain us.

2 Following Beverley McLachlin's lead, John Ralston Saul (*Globe and Mail*, 11 March 2003) offers us "the Canadian experiment" in just these terms. It is not clear how far this is distinctively Canadian, however. Certainly there is a tradition in American jurisprudence, and on its own highest bench, of interpreting American constitutional and social history in the same light.

3 This is a discomfort of which Fenn's version of Christianity will quickly cure the latter, at least (or may do, if they are not misled by his appeal to "religionless Christianity," as if he somehow remained in Bonhoeffer's orbit).

4 An earlier version of this chapter was presented to a conference on religious freedom at Trinity Western University, 8 June 2002.

Of course it is not an easy task to get beyond idols or even
to articulate a form of secularity that is in principle liberated
from them. Fenn's particular attempt might be seen, I think,
as an answer to the challenge laid down by Wilson in the
conclusion to *Religion in Secular Society*. There Wilson wrestles
with the fundamental question of social cohesion raised by the
advance of secularism: "The secular society of the present, in
which religious thinking, practices and institutions, have but
a small part, is none the less the inheritor of values, disposi-
tions and orientations from the religious past. The completely
secularized society has not yet existed. Whether indeed our
own type of society will effectively maintain public order, without institutional coercion, once the persisting influence of
past religion wanes even further, remains to be seen."[5] The
answer Fenn gives is that social cohesion will arise ultimately
from the levelling effects of a still more courageous icono-
clasm, one that cuts the ground out from under privilege and
prejudice, defeating every exclusionary tendency, including
that of nationalism.

Fenn recognizes that there are those who are unhappy with
such an answer; who find all this a worrisome departure from
the wisdom of experience, if not a cleverly disguised bid for
hegemony by some new and alien god; who, like Durkheim or
Troeltsch or Bellah, think it best to admit that *some* form of
civil religion is inevitable and, indeed, necessary to hold society together.[6] But Fenn knows where his loyalties lie in the war
of the sociologists. Respect for civil religion represents a

---

5 p. 233.

6 The term "civil religion" (which Durkheim did not use and Bellah
   dropped) is even harder to define than are its constituent parts.
   We may employ it, however, to indicate a set of beliefs, symbols,
   and practices – overlapping but not identical to other sets belonging to this or that religion – that serves to sanction or sacralize a
   socio-political entity and identity. It may or may not rest on what
   Eisenach, *Next Religious Establishment,* 58f., 122f., calls a "national
   political theology," but it will entail something analogous to that.

failure of nerve. He warns us against its retrogressive nature, sounding for all the world (however jarring the analogy) like Joshua or Caleb warning Israel at Kadesh not to turn back towards Egypt from the promised land: "I see in whatever vestiges of civil religion survive in the United States a threat to the possibility of a secular society in which individuals, groups, communities, and the nation itself live without illusions of their own uniqueness or superiority and in openness to the possibilities for a global human community."[7]

My own very different thesis is that secularism and civil religion are not, after all, such different creatures, where secularity is understood along the lines that Wilson helped to popularize and that Fenn wishes to radicalize. I will come round later to a defence of this thesis and to the alternative view of secularity I hope to encourage, but I want to make my approach by way of a closer consideration of civil religion, not as we find it in Durkheim's camp – in criticism of which I would join forces with Fenn – but as we find it at its earlier conceptual source. I refer of course to Jean-Jacques Rousseau and, more specifically, to the infamous final chapter of *Du contrat social*.[8] When we have looked again at this widely, if often disingenuously, disowned document we will consider as well another orphaned text, this time of Canadian provenance: the preamble to the Charter of Rights and Freedoms. It will take us some time to get as far as that, however. Preambles are very important, and there is quite a lot to consider in Rousseau, who will provide me with a suitable preamble of my own.

---

7 Fenn, *Beyond Idols*, 12 (cf. Numbers 14:6ff.). On the war of the sociologists see 13ff., while noting that Fenn is indebted to David Martin as well as to Wilson. Compare Baum, *Religion and Alienation*, chap. 7.

8 Fenn scarcely mentions Rousseau in his dispute with the civil religionists, and the civil religionists themselves generally disown Rousseau. But see Cristi's *From Civil to Political Religion*, which views civil religion, whether more or less authoritarian, in terms of a continuum.

ROUSSEAU'S RELIGIOUS TYPOLOGY

One hardly needs to be reminded of the work's famous opening gambit, "Man is born free, and everywhere he is in chains."[9] In the penultimate chapter of Book 4, a chapter entitled "On Civil Religion," Rousseau takes up (in its political dimensions) the religious aspect of man's bondage; that is, he considers religion in its relation both to civil and to international strife. For present purposes we may pass over his superficial and deeply flawed account of the history of political theology, except to demur when faced with his equation of theological with civil intolerance. Though often united (Northern Ireland comes to mind, for instance, or Pakistan, Indonesia, the Sudan, etc.) these two are not "naturally the same thing," as he claims,[10] and the claim is fundamental to his argument. But what is his argument?

Rousseau asserts that Christianity's doctrine of the Two, that is, of a "double seat of authority" – in which a spiritual authority belonging to bishops and priests is distinguished from a material or temporal authority belonging to princes and

---

9 "Gambit," of course, because there is no real evidence that man is born free, in Rousseau's sense of the word. Nor is there any justification for following the social contract theorists in assigning "the origin of political institutions to a mythical agreement among the members of society"; that is, of representing "the whole sphere of political existence, even communal existence, as the invention of man's will" (O'Donovan, *Resurrection and Moral Order*, 129f.; cf. Chapter 4, this volume). This Rousseau also does, though he is critical of the way in which his predecessors handled the matter. See Horowitz and Horowitz, *"Everywhere They Are in Chains,"* chap. 2f.

10 See pp. 423, 438. Unless otherwise noted my quotations from *Du contrat social* (1762) are taken from Gerard Hopkins's translation in *Social Contract: Essays by Locke, Hume and Rousseau* (London: Oxford University Press, 1947), with an introduction by Ernest Barker.

magistrates – "gave rise to a perpetual state of conflict between opposing jurisdictions."[11] It is in this way that Christianity effectively destroyed the hard-won promise of the *pax Romana*, inwardly dividing the loyalties of the citizenry so as to create the conditions for renewed civil strife and, eventually, for wars of religion. His thesis here is that of Thomas Hobbes, of course, and to Hobbes he gives credit for seeing "the evil clearly, and the remedy too"; namely, "that the two heads of the eagle should be united, and that all should be brought into a single political whole, without which no state and no government can ever be firmly established."[12] Rousseau criticizes Hobbes, however, for failing to see that "the arrogant spirit of Christianity is incompatible with his system" and must inevitably undermine the interests and authority of the state, the monarch's headship over the church notwithstanding.[13] In place of such a system Rousseau offers his own alternative, which, mutatis mutandis, modern Canada, like Tony Blair's modern Britain, is arguably in the process of adopting.

Rousseau's alternative is easily understood once we have grasped his basic religious typology. Religion, he says, can be divided into three kinds. First, there is natural religion. This is the religion of man qua man, which for Rousseau means man in his native individuality, considered only in himself and in his vertical relation to his Maker – a relation mediated by

---

11 Ibid., 427.

12 Ibid., 429 (capitalization altered); Compare Hobbes, *De Cive* (1642) and *Leviathan* (1651).

13 Hobbes's constitutional monarch is still an absolute monarch, but even that is an insufficient safeguard against ecclesiastical manipulation. According to Rousseau (429), "It would be easy to prove [to the likes of Pierre Bayle] that no State was ever yet founded save on a basis of religion, and [to a Bishop Warburton] that the Christian law is, fundamentally, more harmful than useful to the firm establishment of the community."

that "divine instinct," conscience.[14] Natural religion is a religion "without temples, without altars, without rites, and strictly
limited to the *inner* worship of the Supreme God, and to the
eternal obligations of morality." It is akin to what Kant would
call "pure religious faith."[15] Second, there is civil religion,
which is the religion of man as a socio-political creature, of
man qua citizen. "Its dogmas, its rites, its forms of worship, are
all prescribed by law," says Rousseau, and its duties and privileges are limited "to the territories in which its altars reign
supreme."[16] Third, there is priestly religion, "which, by giving
to men two sets of laws, two heads, two countries, imposes
upon them two contradictory systems of duty, and makes it
impossible for them to be at the same time devout individuals

14 Rousseau's religious thought, in its inward dimension, turns on
    the Neoplatonist/Augustinian axis of God and the soul, though
    an important shift takes place (under the tutelage of the Savoyard
    Vicar in *Émile*) whereby love for the Good, as an innate feeling,
    as an instinct or compulsion of conscience, is made prior to and
    more fundamental than knowledge of the Good, which is a prod-
    uct of reason. Here is one root of the modern form of alienation
    between feeling (religious or otherwise) and reason.
15 Ibid., 430 (cf. Kant's *Religion within the Limits of Reason Alone*, III).
    Pure religious faith (such as we find in Jesus but not in the later
    church) can find its expression in a social form, but it has "no
    particular relation to the body politic" and "leaves to the laws the
    force which they derive from themselves, and adds nothing to it"
    (432). To that extent, "one of the chief bonds of the social fabric
    remains ineffective"; indeed, it militates against loyalty to the state
    and weans us away "from all merely earthly concerns." Rousseau
    concludes, more pessimistically than Kant: "I know of nothing
    more at odds with the spirit of society."
16 "It is a species of Theocracy in which there is no Pontiff but the
    Prince, no priests but the magistrates." In this type of religion, to
    suffer martyrdom is "to die for one's country"(431).

and good citizens." Of this third type historic Christianity is the prime, but not the only, example.[17]

Now each type, remarks Rousseau, has its faults. "The third is so obviously bad that to demonstrate the fact, though it might be amusing, would be merely a waste of time." Since it "disrupts the social bond of unity" and even sets a man in contradiction to himself, it is at best worthless, at worst dangerously seditious. The first and the second are not without flaw either. The first, just because it is purely inward in orientation, and inclined to the universal or the abstract rather than to the particular and the concrete, may engender apathy in the political sphere; this is particularly true of its Christian form. The second, while generating a laudable devotion to the state and to its juridical and military apparatus – linking "divine worship with a love of the laws" and with a willingness to die for one's country – may at the same time cultivate credulous superstition or an empty ceremonialism, not to speak of nationalistic intolerance, bloody-mindedness, and war. Yet the first and the second, natural religion and civil religion, can have a civilizing influence on each other. Precisely because one is strictly inner or other-worldly, the other strictly outer or this-worldly, because one is strictly private and the other strictly public, it is possible for the two to operate in tandem, without contradiction, each curbing the other's excess and making up its deficit.

Here, then, is Rousseau's alternative. Hobbes, with his Erastian solution, fails to exorcize the demon of mixed or priestly religion, which confuses the sphere of the body and the sphere of the soul, and so corrupts both.[18] But Rousseau, by opting for a combination of natural and civil religion – carefully delineated one from the other – will drive priestly

---

17 Other examples of the third type include "the religion of the Lamas" and of the Japanese.

18 Rousseau might have appealed to Luther here (*Temporal Authority*, 11), though his own dualism is more exaggerated than is Luther's.

religion out of the body politic and send it into the abyss from
which it came.

In any given society a successful exorcism must depend, of
course, upon reforming and conforming actual religions
according to the dictates of this typology: an ambitious task
indeed. But even at the theoretical level success is assured only
in so far as natural and civil religion can be kept apart, thus
preventing any lapse into an ersatz doctrine of the Two. This
creates some difficulties for Rousseau, arising first from the
arbitrary character of civil religion – which, as he admits, is
commonly founded on "errors and lies" – and second from
civil religion's need for a transcendent footing. Civil religion
can get out of hand, in other words, as can natural or private
religion. Both will have to exercise some restraint.

To protect the latter Rousseau employs his principle of
public utility. The state, "not being competent in the affairs of
the other world," can take no official interest in the beliefs or
dogmas of anyone's private religion, "except as they have a
bearing on the morals and duties which the citizen professing
it should hold and perform in dealing with others." In the
words of the Marquis d'Argenson, "In the Republic each man
is perfectly free in all things that do no harm to others."[19] The
exception clause, however, is a significant one, which must not
be overlooked. It heavily qualifies the citizen's freedom of religion. For it is "of considerable concern to the State whether
a citizen profess a religion which leads him to love his duties,"
neglect of those duties being detrimental to all. The state has
no choice, then, but to concern itself with the horizontal, or
ethical, component of natural religion and of the citizen's
private beliefs. That is a point to which we will return, but only
after we have noticed as well that the state (in the form of civil
religion and for the sake of reinforcing the citizen's love of
duty) must trespass even upon the vertical or other-worldly
component of natural religion.

---

19 "This is the unalterable criterion, and it could not be more
    precisely stated," he says in an admiring note (436).

The incursion of civil religion into the transcendent sphere is mandated by the citizen's need for special motivation to honour the social contract – a device that, however necessary, unnaturally constrains human beings – and by the state's need to exercise the ultimate sanctions in defence of that contract. Before indicating the incursion's theological coordinates, however, we ought to observe that it is undertaken with a disclaimer. Civil religion, says Rousseau, requires "a purely civil profession of faith, the articles of which it behoves the Sovereign to fix, not with the precision of religious dogmas, but treating them as a body of social sentiments without which no one can be either a good citizen or a faithful subject." What Rousseau means by *sentimens de sociabilité* is beliefs that are held out of devotion to the needs of the state rather than to truth itself or to God as the author of truth.[20] The one who refuses to profess them is guilty, then, not of theological error but, rather, of a lack of social sense and, more seriously, of a lack of love for the laws, for justice, for duty. Such a one is subject to banishment or exile – to political excommunication – for just that reason. As for the one who makes his profession but demonstrates unbelief by his deeds, he is deserving of death. "For he has committed the greatest of all crimes, that of lying before the law."

Now the articles of civil religion, in so far as it attempts this incursion, are few and tersely stated. They will not support and must not be made the object of philosophical exposition or theological commentary, lest they be mistaken for pure theology and become the source of civil strife.

The positive clauses are: – the existence of a powerful, intelligent, beneficent and bountiful God: the reality of the life to come: the reward of the just, and the punishment of evil-doers: the sanctity of the Social Contract and of the Laws. The negative element I would confine to a single article: – intolerance, for that belongs to the creeds I have excluded.[21]

---

20 See his note, 437.

21 Ibid., 438.

Over against the enthusiasm of priestly religion (particularly Christianity) for the proliferation of dogma and of doctrinal controversy, we may well admire Rousseau's restraint. But we must also observe a rather obvious shortcoming. If these "sentiments" of civil religion are not susceptible of any precise definition, if indeed it is not clear that they refer to anything actually transcendent,[22] then it is also not clear how they can motivate the citizen. More seriously, it is not clear how they might serve to secure the character of the state to which the citizen is meant to be loyal. The "God" who stands in back of the state, guaranteeing its right and power to enforce the social contract, may be none other than a projection of the state itself. The power, intelligence, beneficence, and justice of this God may be none other than the power, intelligence, beneficence, and justice of the state itself – such as it is or may become. This redoubling of the state's authority by the deployment of theological language, in which it is not permitted to subject the claims of the state to any authentically theological analysis, effectively renders the state itself infallible. Either that, or it leaves the state open to the citizen's contempt.

If, on the other hand, we allow that the incursion of civil religion into the transcendent sphere of natural religion is something more than mere appearance – if instead of an appropriation of theological language we are faced rather with an occupation, however limited, of theological territory – well, then, have we not reverted to mixed religion? We may not have a doctrine of the Two, but we do have an overlap between the private and the public, between the eternal and the temporal, an overlap in which the possibility of serious conflict again arises, unless the state allocates to itself the final word about both. What becomes here of the individual and her religious conscience, however it is formed, if it is at odds with the corporate will and with the determination of the state? Arguably the doctrine of the Two, with all its potential

---

22 Are they, to use a Kantian term, simply "necessary myths"?

for conflict, has simply been reproduced by Rousseau in terms of the individual and the state, or conscience and law.[23]

Indeed, whichever tack we take in our reading of Rousseau, we come pretty much to the same place; namely, to a reinforcing of the religious hegemony of the state as the only possible answer to the weakness he perceived in Hobbes's proposal. In matters religious Rousseau forges not freedom but, rather, new and stronger chains. This conclusion is borne out by his exposition (for he does offer one) of the lone negative article of his civil religion – the intolerance of intolerance. This paradoxical article, which has proved to have the most staying power in Western political culture, may be paired with his famous claim that those who "refuse to obey the general will must be constrained to do so by the entire body; which means only that he will be forced to be free."[24] Our concern here, however, is simply with its connection to the religious hegemony of the state.

Admittedly, talk of the religious hegemony of the state would seem to Rousseau to be an anachronism. Did the Thirty Years War and the Peace of Westphalia not bring about a new pluralism, in which there could no longer be "any exclusive national religion"? In the new situation must society not learn to "tolerate all creeds which show tolerance to others, so long

---

23 Horowitz and Horowitz conclude that "the ideal of free and equal individuals making the laws of society their own, and their own laws the laws of the society, is incompatible with civil religion." They add: "In the *Social Contract* Rousseau cannot see how such individuals can come into existence, but he does come to see this as *the* problem to be addressed." Afterwards, in *Émile*, we have a figure "who is not caught up in anything like the civil religion" (*"Everywhere They Are in Chains,"* 90f.). From this perspective, however, it may be asked whether we are not dealing rather with a project that runs aground on the older philosophical problem of the one and the many, in its social form.

24 *On the Social Contract,* I.7 (Masters, 55). See editorial note 37 (Masters, 138), the thesis of which is not entirely convincing.

as their dogmas contain nothing at variance with the duties of citizens"? But the exception clauses are again decisive. I promised that we would return to the second of these, and we will, but let us first dispose of the first. Rousseau himself does not permit us to miss the point: "But anyone who dares to say 'Outside the Church there can be no salvation,' should be banished from the State, unless the State be the Church and the Prince the Pontiff. Such a dogma is good only where the government is theocratic. In any other it is pernicious."[25] Why is it, then, that Rousseau admits as permissible only those religions that do not show intolerance to others – that is to say, that do not lay claim to absolute truth? Why is it that he makes of the rest seditious *superstitiones* that ought to be illegal, unless, as he says, they *are* the state? Just because the state, as he conceives it, has a prior claim to absolute truth.

Of course that is not the reason Rousseau explicitly gives; one might even suggest that nothing could be further from his mind. The reason he gives is that exclusivist religions like Roman Catholicism, which pretend to offer unique access to absolute truth, inevitably undermine the integrity of the *respublica*.[26]

Those who draw a distinction between civil and theological intolerance are, in my opinion, guilty of error. The two things are inseparable. It is impossible to live in peace with those whom we believe to be damned. To love them would be to hate God who punishes them. It is essential that they be either converted or punished. Wherever theological intolerance enters it cannot but have an effect on civil life, and when that happens, the Sovereign is no longer sovereign, even in temporal affairs. From then on the priests are the real masters, the kings no more than their officers.

---

25 The reference which follows to Henry IV, as a prince with no brains, brings us full circle at the end of Chapter 8 (439f.) to Hobbes's mistake.

26 Thus also Locke, in his *Letter Concerning Toleration* (1689), though the case is differently argued.

We must not be fooled by Rousseau's sleight of hand, however, or by his special pleading.[27] It is not merely that he tries to pass off Christian heresy as Christian orthodoxy, producing a strictly sectarian caricature of church teaching – as if the church had nothing to say about the love of God for all people, which Christians must emulate if they hope to be accounted children of God; or about the eschatological reserve in divine judgment, which makes today a "day of salvation" not damnation; or about the fact that divine judgment belongs to God and to God alone. It is not even that, when this caricature is set aside, there is no obvious connection between theological intolerance of the sort that is found in the maxim *extra ecclesiam non sit salus* and civil intolerance. No, the sleight of hand is this: Rousseau himself is guilty of the very charge he falsely levels at the church. His attack on the church, whose theological intolerance "naturally" leads to civil intolerance, serves as cover for the fact that civil intolerance is just what he is calling for. It also serves as cover for the fact that the civil intolerance he himself advocates follows indeed from theological intolerance, a theological intolerance of a quite different and reprehensible sort – the sort that banishes Roman Catholics, say, simply for being Roman Catholics.

Let me explain. The problem with the *extra ecclesiam nulla salus* is not that it generates civil intolerance but, rather, that it limits and qualifies the state by appeal to a higher truth and a higher authority. Since the church stakes its claim not merely as an invisible but also as a visible body, it disallows the state's own claim to absolute authority over things bodily and public.[28] Rousseau's concession that the state is not competent in the affairs of the *other* world – a concession partially withdrawn in the positive articles of his civil religion – is not enough for the church. "Outside the church there is no

---

27 Does he himself not appeal here to "the reward of the just, and the punishment of evildoers" (438)?

28 In Rousseau's words, "the sacred cult ... is without any true bond of union with the body of the State" (427).

salvation," when said with reference to a visible and identifiable society, means that the state is not permitted to regard itself as the saviour of man in *this* world either. Rousseau recognizes this when he remarks that the sovereign is then not truly sovereign, even in temporal affairs. To put it another way, if Jesus is Lord (as the church believes) not only over some other world but also, in some way, over this world, then Caesar's own lordship has been qualified. Rendering unto Caesar the things that are Caesar's may mean, inter alia, that one must pay one's taxes or serve in Caesar's army, but it will not mean ceding to Caesar authority in all things temporal or even in all things pertaining to the public good. Caesar will be subject to scrutiny, to criticism, and even to resistance in so far as he acts in a way opposed to the truth and the authority of Jesus. For authority rests on competence and Caesar's competence – set against that of the resurrected Christ – is distinctly limited.[29]

Rousseau's reaction to all of this is to insist that people who hold such beliefs are not fit to participate in the state. It does not matter that these people do not believe that the church is, or ought to be, the state. Indeed, they would be excused if only it were actually so, in their particular case, that the church were the state and the state the church. Why? Because (as we have seen) the state's authority in matters of public welfare must be absolute or it is no authority at all. The state's claim, as Rousseau would have it, is not only absolute but absolutist.[30] It brooks no competition, and since it does not and cannot concern itself with "the fate of its members in the life to come," it

---

29 This resistance ultimately takes the form of martyrdom – in the Christian sense of the word, not that of civil religion or of some forms of Islamic religion – as, for example, in the case of St Sergius (d. 303), who was completely wanting, obviously, in the matter of *sentimens de sociabilité.*

30 Rousseau is not, of course, advocating tyranny; it is Christianity that, if taken in pure doses, would lead finally to tyranny (432ff.). Yet even the Islamic states disappoint him here (427f.).

refuses even in this life to be tempered by the eschatological reservations that characterize the church's claim.

So much, then, for the first exception clause. The state will tolerate only creeds that are not intolerant of others as religious intolerance is a prerogative of the state, and of the state alone. The second exception clause reinforces the state's religious hegemony: creeds will be tolerated only "so long as their dogmas contain nothing at variance with the duties of citizens."[31] Now the full force of this exception can only be felt when stock is taken of the unity between the vertical and horizontal, or theological and ethical, dimensions of religion in historic Christianity. As William Cavanaugh observes, religion is there understood as "a habit of appropriate disposition of body and soul toward God, a habit which governs the person's behaviour without regard to distinctions of 'public' and 'private.'" For someone like Aquinas, "*religio* – as external and bodily and not merely interior – presupposes an entire context of communal practices by which the person is bound to others in the Body of Christ."

At the dawn of modernity, however, moves are made that begin to undo this unity, depriving religion of its social character, internalizing it.

In the late-fifteenth and the sixteenth century ... "religion" in the modern sense is created as a universal human impulse buried within the recesses of the individual heart. As religion is therefore removed from its specific ecclesial context, Christianity becomes for the first time "a religion," one of a genus of religions, a system of beliefs rather than a virtue located within a set of theological claims and practices which assume a social form called Church. The crucial move ... is the separation of religion and Church (unless the Church is absorbed by the state, as in Hobbes). If religion was to remain as

---

31 Ibid., 439. Or, as he puts it earlier (437), it will take no particular interest in them "except as they have a bearing on the morals and duties which the citizen professing it should hold and perform in dealing with others."

a practice of *religare* at all, it would serve only to bind the individual to the state.[32]

In this way the modern state is made to compete directly not with its mediaeval counterpart, nor yet with the individual, but with the church. *Extra respublicam nulla salus?* is the question raised by the political tradition from Hobbes to Rousseau, as Cavanaugh rightly perceives.

By implication, then, the occupation of theological territory by the state is not partial but complete. By allocating all critical community-building functions to itself – witness marriage, for example, the secularization of which Rousseau thinks crucial to the state's cause[33] – the state does not so much make room for religious pluralism as *nationalize* religion once again, on the principle, if not in the fashion, of the ancient imperial cult. It rejects the right of church or synagogue or temple to order the lives of its members in any politically relevant way; instead, it clears the way for a civil religion that binds the citizen exclusively to the state, and to the state as supreme.

Let it be added, in conclusion to my preamble, that all of this is possible only on the basis of the entrenched body/soul dualism of this period. That dualism helps to account for the

---

32 William Cavanaugh, "The City: Beyond Secular Parodies," 191, in Milbank, Pickstock, and Ward, *Radical Orthodoxy*, 182–200. I am much indebted to this provocative piece, though I cannot offer a more direct engagement with it here.

33 See the extended note on 438f., which is still highly germane, even if some today might question his assumption that the state "could not continue were it composed only of bastards." The battle Rousseau describes there has gone largely in favour of the state, which in some cases, is now busily reinventing marriage on an entirely different template. As Wilson, *Religion in Secular Society*, 224f., says, society will no longer "brook interference of the traditional kind in ... matters relating to marriage and birth" or education. But compare Chapters 3 and 4 (this volume), which challenge the allocation to the state of such basic community-building functions.

fact that "the real duties of religion" are carefully detached from "human institutions" such as the church and relocated in the private realm of conscience.[34] But of course they cannot remain detached for long, and the institutional body to which they are reattached is that of the state. Today it is customary to charge mediaeval Christianity with such a dualism. So far as there is any truth to this charge (and there is some) it points to a departure, under Greek and Persian influences, from the obvious implications of Judeo-Christian belief in bodily resurrection.[35] But Rousseau, like other Enlightenment thinkers, holds no such belief. What he offers us in *Du contrat social* is a dualism more exaggerated than anything to be found in the Judeo-Christian tradition. And in the collapse or overcoming of that dualism a new and more sinister form of mixed religion arises. For, truth be told, Rousseau's civil religion – like Hobbes's – *is* priestly religion under a new guise. Only in Rousseau it is perhaps more evident, if further evidence is needed, that there has indeed been a change in the priesthood, hence also in the law.[36]

SECULARISM AS THE SUBLIMATION OF CIVIL RELIGION

To recapitulate: Rousseau's religious typology entrenches one of the fundamental principles of modern political discourse; namely, that the positive religions must withdraw from civic

---

34 The quoted phrases are from *Émile* (also published in 1762), again from the Savoyard Vicar. James Livingston's (*Modern Christian Thought*, 1:40ff.) account of this relocation is typical in overlooking the underlying soul/body dualism, which is now transfiguring itself into belief/conduct and person/act dualisms that threaten to do considerable harm in jurisprudence especially (though the distinctions as such are vital, of course).

35 On which see, for example, Wright, *The Resurrection of the Son of God.*

36 Compare Hebrews 7:12.

life. Building on the contributions of Hobbes and Locke,[37] Rousseau refuses to allow the kind of overlap between church and state in which the two cooperate, but also contend, for the common good. The church (or any other religious institution) is to be tolerated by the state only in so far as it relinquishes its claim on the public square. Authentic religion can have, as Kant later says, no *Zustand*, or public status, being an inward affair.[38] But in a political sense even the positive religions (which seek to cultivate authentic religion through their symbolic cults) can have no public status. Public status, according to Rousseau, is something that only civil religion can enjoy.[39]

This principle, so far as it concerns withdrawal or relinquishing, has garnered wide support in Western societies from the late eighteenth century to the present, albeit usually in a more moderate or patient form than the one it takes in Rousseau. On the other hand, Rousseau's notion of civil religion – briefly and tragically incarnated during *le Directoire* – has increasingly been rejected in favour of something called "secular" society and the secular state. To this subject we may now return.

Secular society is generally seen as the product of withdrawal, whether willing or forced. The term "secularization" refers first of all to the expropriation of ecclesiastical properties in sixteenth-century England or eighteenth-century

37 Not to speak of Grotius, of course, and numerous others. See Ernest Barker's introduction to *Social Contract*, xxxv ff. On Grotius, compare O'Donovan and O'Donovan, *From Irenaeus to Grotius*, 787ff.

38 *Religion* III, Division 2.

39 We cannot stop to consider Kant's alternative, the ethical commonwealth. As for Locke, he proposes nothing in the way of a shared or public religious enterprise. Religion may be cordoned off from public affairs; in so far as it agrees to its privatization it is no threat to the state and is of no concern to the state. This is the inspiration for the United States' "wall of separation" tradition, from Jefferson to John Rawls.

France, for example, and hence of economic and political power. What had been devoted through the church, at least ostensibly, to the service of things eternal would now be devoted by the state to the service of things temporal. But this form of secularization was accompanied, whether slowly (as in England) or more rapidly (as in France), by a more general process of sweeping out the public square, removing the detritus left by centuries of Christian influence on Western culture.[40] Some of this detritus was symbolic; some belonged to the intellectual fabric of the universities; some belonged to the legal traditions or to civic standards.[41] This sweeping of the public square was and remains a haphazard business since many have not regarded the cultural artefacts of this influence as detritus, and few have been prepared to argue that these artefacts are altogether harmful to society or altogether dispensable. Nevertheless, secularization came to indicate, in Bryan Wilson's words, the broader process "whereby religious thinking, practice and institutions lose social significance."[42]

This loss of significance could again be willing or forced. That is, it could be a conscious adaptation of religious authorities

---

40 For an analysis of the corresponding process in the United States, see Smith, *The Secular Revolution.*

41 In France both the symbolic and the practical were taken into account from the start. In 1795, when the worst excesses of the Revolution's religious persecution (and somewhat farcical religious experimentation) were already passing, and expropriated churches were being returned, "the public announcement of service, as by the ringing of bells, was forbidden." The clergy were also "forbidden to interfere in the matter of the registry of vital statistics" and so on. See *The New Schaff-Herzog Encyclopedia of Religious Knowledge*, vol. 4 (New York: Funk and Wagnalls, 1909), 387; compare Aston, *Religion and Revolution in France, 1780–1804.*

42 Wilson, *Religion in Secular Society*, xiv. Obviously there is much more to be said than this. One who has been exploring the nuances of the secularization process, in its positive as well as in its negative aspects, is Charles Taylor. For an overview of his findings, including his Gifford Lectures, see Smith, *Charles Taylor*, chap. 5.

and institutions to the redefinition of the public square that follows from the redefinition of authentic religion, or it could be a grudging retreat in the face of open hostility to ecclesial influence – a demoralizing defeat in a *Kulturkampf* waged on a variety of fronts, from parlour to parliament. Either way, "secular society" and "the secular state" gradually came to mean the society and the state as liberated from any and every imposition of religion, and from any positing of the sacred, or even of faith in the sacred, as a category with public relevance.[43] This can be demonstrated easily in the sphere of law, to give one vital illustration.

In Canada an important turning point came in 1967, when the Honourable Pierre Elliott Trudeau became minister of justice in the Pearson government. The move to decriminalize certain bodily acts and to alter family law was not an especially daring one, given developments in Britain, but it could not be undertaken lightly. Trudeau's famous statement in the election campaign of the following year, that "the state has no place in the bedrooms of the nation," was an act of consciousness-raising with respect to the process of secularization we are considering.[44] The distinction between sin and crime to which he appealed is an essential one, with a history as long as that of Christendom, to which in fact it belongs. But its deployment at the time, arguably, and its subsequent interpretation, certainly, represent for Canada a nodal point in the long process of Western society's rejection of Christendom and its doctrine of the Two. Sin now became a matter of private concern only, a concern mediated (if mediated at all) by priest or by therapist, of no interest to the state. Crime, likewise, became a

---

43 Obviously I am not using "sacred" in quite the sense, or with the breadth of reference, introduced earlier by Fenn.

44 It may also prove to be a turning point in the history of marriage in Canada. For if the bedrooms of the nation are of no concern at all to the state, neither is marriage, understood as (inter alia) a sexual union. At present, however, Trudeau's maxim is being undermined by the insistence on same-sex marriage.

strictly public matter in the definition of which the church qua church has no vested interest. Curiously enough, the literary critic, for example, may be assumed to have (or may be asked to take) such an interest, as in the recent John Robin Sharpe pornography case. But not the church or the synagogue or the mosque or the temple.[45]

And yet – let me not paint too stark a picture – church and synagogue may act as friends of the court and often do. Indeed in 1982 the Right Honourable Pierre Trudeau gave Canada a Charter of Rights and Freedoms, which, if its preamble is anything to go by, implies that church and synagogue (etc.) may be regarded as quite special friends of the country and of its courts. For Canada has "God" in its Charter, as everyone knows. It may be the case that "God" showed up at the last minute.[46] It may also be true that it is less and less clear to Canadians who or what this God is or can hope to do from there, but Canada cannot be regarded as a strictly secular country, in the popular sense of the term, so long as its constitutional documents, not to speak of its anthem, continue to offer this sanctuary for the sacred. In this Canada is quite typical, of course. Britain and the United States, for

---

45 It should be noted, however, that in the matter of abortion – legalization of which was buried deep in the bowels of Trudeau's 1969 Omnibus Bill, C-150 – a category between sin and crime was established. Abortion might be one and not the other, or both, or neither. But it could *not* be either strictly private or strictly public. Mediating here in a priestly way was a panel of three doctors, who would decide the appropriateness, and hence the legality, of the act.

46 "Whereas Canada is founded upon principles that recognize the supremacy of God and the rule of law" was a late addition to the Charter (see David Brown, "Freedom From or Freedom For? Religion as a Case Study in Defining the Content of *Charter* Rights," *UBC Law Review* 33 [2000]: 561, n.52; following P.W. Hogg, *Canada Act 1982 Annotated* (Toronto: Carswell, 1986). It is also much briefer than its predecessor in the 1960 Canadian Bill of Rights.

example, whose secularisms have different roots and come in different flavours, still have public spaces of this sort for "God." Among prominent Western states that is the norm.[47]

De jure, then, it is not correct to say that countries like Canada are secular, if secular is taken to mean, in an absolute rather than a relative way, "not concerned with or related to religion."[48] All the sweeping notwithstanding, this cannot be said de facto either. Religion (*pace* Fenn) is by no means disappearing as an influential element of Canadian life. On the other hand, it *has* been said de jure that Canada is secular in the sense we have been discussing, the sense in which "religious thinking, practice, and institutions" are deprived of public significance. God-talk has, in the view of many of our judges, no place in law. As David Brown observes in the *University of British Columbia Law Review,* the British Columbia Court of Appeal has gone so far as to describe the words of the preamble as "a dead letter" into which that court has "no authority to breathe life" – an act of resurrection, it says, which only the Supreme Court of Canada could hope to bring about.[49] Certainly this miracle was not attempted in the court

---

47 The European Union may not follow this norm, though John Paul II (*Ecclesia in Europa,* 28 June 2003, §114) has appealed to it to do so. As for modern America, see Witte Jr, *Religion and the American Constitutional Experiment,* 231ff.

48 The other meanings provided by the *Collins English Dictionary,* 3rd ed. (Glasgow: HarperCollins, 1994) – "of or relating to worldly as opposed to sacred things," or "not within the control of the church" – more obviously trade on the relativity of the secular and the religious, a relativity that cannot be missed in a perusal of the *OED* entry.

49 p. 562 (quoting *R. v. Sharpe,* 1999, B.C.J. no. 1555, §§78–80, per Southin J.A.). By an irony that may or may not be conscious, the court's statement here is fraught with biblical allusions – to Genesis, the Gospels, and the epistles of Paul. Apparently these biblical texts, though somewhat more ancient than the Charter, have not suffered the fate of its preamble. On the metaphorical level, at least, they are alive and well.

led by Chief Justice Lamer, who in the *Rodriguez* case opined
that the Charter had established "the essentially secular
nature of Canadian society"; by which remark he apparently
meant to reinforce his claim that "philosophical and theological" and even moral considerations were out of place in the
court's deliberation.[50] It can be no surprise, then, that in
acting as a friend to the court most religious groups and
institutions are very hesitant to incorporate into their briefs
content that is overtly theological.

It is not only as a theologian but also as a Canadian that I
think this position untenable. Either Canada is, or is not,
"founded upon principles that recognize the supremacy of
God and the rule of law." Either it is, or is not, committed to
the notion that divine worship is linked – one way or another
– to "a love of the laws," and a love of the laws to divine
worship. Either Canada is, or is not, prepared to affirm, in the
words of its Bill of Rights, "that men and institutions remain
free only when freedom is founded upon respect for moral

---

50 Dissenting in *Rodriguez v. British Columbia* [1993] 3 S.C.R. 519,
Lamer writes at p. 553: "Can the right to choose at issue here,
that is the right to choose suicide, be described as an advantage
of which the appellant is being deprived? In my opinion, the
Court should answer this question without reference to the philosophical and theological considerations fuelling the debate on
the morality of suicide or euthanasia. It should consider the question before it from a legal perspective ... while keeping in mind
that the *Charter* has established the essentially secular nature of
Canadian society and the central place of freedom of conscience
in the operation of our institutions. As Dickson J. said in *Big
M Drug Mart, supra*, at p. 336: 'A truly free society is one which
can accommodate a wide variety of beliefs, diversity of tastes and
pursuits, customs and codes of conduct.'" Lamer thus appears to
suggest a far-reaching principle, one that would have ·pleased
d'Argenson: a secular society is a free society because it is not
beholden to any vision of the good other than the liberty of its
citizens in all things that do no harm to others.

and spiritual values and the rule of law."[51] If it is, then every-thing that follows the "Whereas" of the Charter preamble, including the very concept of the rule of law, is subject to theological interpretation. But if it is not – that is, if Canada has discovered that it is not in fact so founded or that it does not wish to continue resting upon this foundation – then the "Whereas" clause must be modified or replaced, as some have proposed, or else the authority and intelligibility of the Charter itself must become doubtful.[52]

Now I want to put it to you that the struggle between a theological reading of the Charter (prima facie the obvious one) and a "secular" reading (the currently prevailing one) is itself a religious struggle. This claim is anything but obvious and must be defended. In doing so, of course, I am intending also to expound and defend the subtitle I have given this

---

51 The dispute over the nature and force of the 1960 Bill of Rights (see, e.g., *R. v. Big M Drug Mart Ltd.* [1985] 1 S.C.R. 295, pp. 305ff.) does not materially affect my point here, though it deserves a discussion I cannot afford it. For historical background see George Egerton's "The Canadian Bill of Rights and the Making of Religious Pluralism" (forthcoming) and "Trudeau, God and the Canadian Constitution," in Lyons and Die, *Rethinking Church, State, and Modernity*, 90–112.

52 Simply striking the preamble will not do; all hermeneutical guidance would then be lost, leaving the country at the mercy of the ideological waves that flow through the universities and law schools. But answer must be given to the charge that it is incoherent as it stands (see Brown, "Freedom From, or Freedom For?" 56off.), which appears to rest on the claim that belief in God cannot be made the foundation for the freedoms of conscience and religion (sec. 2.a) since such freedoms must also apply to those who do *not* believe in God. The answer is: Non sequitur; those who believe in God may be able to provide better warrant for such freedoms, even for those who do not believe in God, than can the latter. More serious is the charge that the preamble is too terse to be of service, a problem to which we will return.

section – "secularism as the sublimation of civil religion" – and the thesis I put forward in the introduction.

My first point is related to that made by Brown and by several other contributors to the same issue of the *UBC Law Review*, who focus our attention on the sleight of hand performed by the advocates of secularism; namely, the pretence that a secularist point of view is philosophically and theologically neutral, that its rationality is equally accessible to all, and as such quintessentially public, by virtue of its eschewal of all faith-based commitments or presuppositions.[53] It is indeed astonishing that so many of our best minds in law and in public life are practised in this dubious manœuvre, which has been challenged often enough, and with sufficient erudition, to make plain how irresponsible and unconvincing it is. There is no such thing as a point of view – certainly not one sufficiently comprehensive to survey or to organize a society – that is either philosophically or theologically neutral. The civil religionists and the communitarians are right about this, and the purveyors of "liberal neutrality" are wrong.[54] Moreover, every point of view is adopted as an act of commitment, in which there is an element of trust, precisely in so far as it is adopted.

---

53 There is an irony here that should not go unnoticed. The formative thinkers of the Western tradition, especially the Platonists, thought that the quintessentially public – that is, doctrine accessible to those who lacked philosophical gifts and commitment – was not properly rational. One of the most controversial claims, then, of early Christian apologists like Justin Martyr (a convert from Platonism) was that the highest truth, the truth of the divine Logos itself, had been made publicly accessible via the incarnation. Which is to say, to combine "public" with "truth" or "reason" was no longer to produce an oxymoron: not because of the *exclusion* of faith but because of the *possibility* of faith in a Logos that had put itself within the reach of the common person.

54 Compare Kymlicka, "Liberal Individualism and Liberal Neutrality," *Ethics* 99 [1989]: 883ff.; and Kymlicka, *Contemporary Political Philosophy*, 2nd ed.

No finite being can see reality whole. One cannot even see the ground under one's own feet, and yet one must stand somewhere in order to see anything at all. That standing, that adopting (*optare*) of a *pou sto* and hence of a point of view, is always therefore an act of commitment that entails a form of trust. This is no less true of the secularist than of anyone else, though in as much as the trust or faith of the secularist corresponds both formally and materially to its own object, it is different in kind from that of the Christian, say, which is different again from that of the Muslim, for example.[55]

The Charter is perfectly right to acknowledge this principle implicitly, by means of its preamble, and to make explicit the joint object of its trust. It does not, like many of our judges, politicians, and journalists, put its trust in something called

---

55 Different in kind, rather than merely in species. In "Notes towards a (Re)definition of the 'Secular,'" *UBC Law Review* 33 (2000): 546, Iain Benson also speaks of kinds, when he concludes: "Those who seek to educate and/or convince judges through legal argument should now speak of the 'secular' in a way that suggests it is a realm of faith amongst many other kinds of faith in a pluralistic society." I wonder, however, whether he does not mean species. Faith, as the word is used in his article, means a position or perspective based on "metaphysical assertions that we do not empirically prove" (519). It can be applied univocally to atheists and to Christians, though atheists and Christians believe quite different things. Benson's argument is sound and ought to be heeded both by anti-religious secularists and by those who are still inclined to defend religion by pleading for the rights of "people of faith," as if there were people *without* faith (and, worse, as if being without faith were somehow the norm, just as the phrase "people of colour" implies that white is the norm). It would be a mistake to use the word in this way exclusively, however, for that would concede too much to the secularism Benson is rejecting. "Faith" has another and deeper sense, one that is ontological as well as epistemological. Here faith is not a necessity of creaturely finitude but a possibility created by a specific redemptive act of God. On this level one may indeed want to speak of people of faith.

Canadian values (not easily defined where anything more complicated than ice hockey is in view) or in that great Enlightenment abstraction, Reason, which has of course its own theological overtones.[56] No, it chooses "God" and "the rule of law." This it does in continuity with a tradition extending back to the foundations of Christendom and in tacit recognition of the fact that one feature of legitimate governance is "sufficient identification with the tradition of the community," which in the case of Canada does indeed have its deepest roots in the Christian civilization of Europe.[57] Its framers might of course have opted to ignore this feature and to introduce a quite radical discontinuity – performing in political and juridical philosophy something like the substitution, in the great flag flap, of the maple leaf for the royal ensign. But here too they would have had both to make their substitution and to defend it as sufficiently continuous with the Canadian tradition, in spite of the evident discontinuity. This they chose not to do.

Today's secularists are attempting such a substitution, however. The criticism being levelled at them is that they are not honestly acknowledging the nature of their action or of their proposed substitution. The ordered relation of the objects of trust in the Charter preamble, "the supremacy of God and the rule of law," suggests at least this: that the latter, as we have traditionally enjoyed it, is hard to account for, to interpret, or to sustain without reference to the former. Otherwise put, support for the rule of law is for the Charter the most immediately (though hardly the only) relevant feature of the theistic heritage of the founders of our nation. In so far as this relevance is denied, the denial ought to rest on careful historical analysis, an analysis that will not be able to avoid philosophical and theological modes of thought and that will have to overcome a great deal of evidence to the

---

56 "The very voice of God," as the Cambridge Platonist and Latitudinarian, Benjamin Whichcote, put it.

57 See O'Donovan, *Desire of the Nations,* 129. Compare Mr Justice Belzil's remarks, as noted in *R. v. Big M Drug Mart Ltd.,* 310f.

contrary.[58] In so far as this relevance is allowed, but the theistic heritage is said to be relevant *no longer* by virtue of fundamental alterations in and to the nation, other equally difficult burdens of proof will have to be shouldered. First, it will have to be shown that those alterations are (1) real and identifiable, (2) democratically and constitutionally legitimate, and (3) more or less settled. This cannot be done by mere assertion, as the critics point out, but must be done by public argument. Second, that which *is* now relevant will have to be specified, and its ability to sustain the rule of law will have to be demonstrated. If it threatens, or promises to alter in any important respect, the meaning of "the rule of law," this too will have to be addressed. The nature of its own philosophical or theological acts of trust will have to be acknowledged; its own dogmas will have to be declared. The substitute, in other words, must be seen for what it is and subjected to a close scrutiny.

I pause to acknowledge, so as not myself to be guilty of sleight of hand, that I am here assuming a great deal epistemologically (hence also philosophically and theologically) that cannot be safely assumed today. In my own defence I will remark only that those who wish to retain the rule of law in anything like its traditional form have no choice but to make a good many of these assumptions with me – whether or not they can do so with consistency.[59] But why would I describe

---

58 On which see again O'Donovan and O'Donovan, *From Irenaeus to Grotius.*

59 One of the most disturbing examples of determined *in*consistency can be found in the S.C.C. ruling on *Ross v. New Brunswick School District No. 15* (1996, 1 S.C.R. 825), which includes the following passage (cited by Brown, "Freedom From or Freedom For?" 602, from §36): "Ours is a free society built upon a foundation of diversity of views; it is also a society that seeks to accommodate this diversity to the greatest extent possible. Such accommodation reflects an adherence to the principle of equality, valuing all divergent views equally and recognizing the contribution that a wide range of beliefs may make in the search for truth. However, to

the contest between a theological and a "secular" reading of the Charter or, more broadly, between the worldview of Christendom and ·the worldview of contemporary political secularism, as a religious one? Does secularism not entail a distancing of the state from religion? Is this distancing not essential if the state is to perform the role that the inventors of pluralism long ago assigned to it; namely, that of keeping peace between the gods?[60]

---

give protection to views that attack and condemn the views, beliefs and practices of others is to undermine the principle that all views deserve equal protection and muzzles the voice of truth." We may pass over the bizarre reference to a "foundation" composed of divergent views. Even more disturbing is the notion that the search for truth can be conducted by "valuing all divergent views equally." This could be redeemed, perhaps, if it were made to mean only that all views deserve a hearing. But having been heard, of course, they will require critical examination if the search for truth is to proceed. They may even need to be attacked and condemned as incoherent or otherwise injurious to the truth. They will certainly *not* be valued equally. To suggest that they might be – worse, that anyone refusing to do so muzzles the voice of truth – is simply absurd. But this absurdity is an echo of Rousseau's "if anyone dares to say, *extra ecclesiam nulla salus...*"

60 The origins of pluralism lie in the writings of the contractarians, who invented it as a means of neutralizing religion's critical capacity vis-à-vis the state. To achieve this goal it was necessary to pretend that the so-called wars of religion were just that. (See William Cavanaugh, "'A Fire Strong Enough to Consume the House': The Wars of Religion and the Rise of the State," *Modern Theology* 11. 4 [1995]: 397–420). It also became necessary to pretend that pluralism is intrinsically valuable, though Teilhard, *Future of Man*, 46, grasped the larger strategy, evident already in Kant and in Hegel, when he looked ahead to the eventual cessation of "regression into plurality": "Pluralism, far from being the ultimate end of evolution, is merely a first outspreading whose gradual shrinkage displays the true curve of Nature's proceedings." This homogenizing pluralism demands as its counterpart the "procedural republic" criticized by Sandel in *Democracy's Discontent.*

And to be effective at this must the state not adopt a studied neutrality towards religious beliefs? Must it not insist, more strenuously than did Rousseau, that it has no theological interests of its own?

Any defence of secularism and of liberal neutrality is likely to follow these lines. It will be protested that liberal secularism, unlike supersessionist secularism,[61] is neither religious nor anti-religious. It is an honest response to the pluralist reality that now confronts us and to the fact that equality rights preclude the privileging of any particular worldview. Are we not all committed to equality? Does this not necessitate some form of the (falsely maligned) "procedural republic"? Surely it is not possible to rank differing conceptions of the good, or to impose such a ranking, without violating the principle of equality?[62] Quite so – where the principle of equality is not one commitment among others but is itself identified as the highest possible common commitment, indeed, as itself the highest attainable public good. But of course this *is* a ranking, and it is not so much agreed as imposed. It is imposed over against the ranking that is alluded to in the Charter preamble and actually evident in the preamble to the Bill of Rights:

The Parliament of Canada, affirming that the Canadian Nation is founded upon principles that acknowledge the supremacy of God, the dignity and worth of the human person and the position of the family in a society of free men and free institutions; Affirming also that men and institutions remain free only when freedom is founded upon respect for moral and spiritual values and the rule of law...

---

61 I employ here the terminology laid out in Farrow, "Three Meanings of Secular," *First Things* 133 (May 2003): 20ff. Supersessionist secularism is of the "religion is *passé*" variety. See below on the third or eschatological type.

62 Thus Robert Brown, for example, in Goodin and Pettit, *Companion to Contemporary Political Philosophy*, 111f., (parrying Sandel's attack on the Rawlsian tradition in *Liberalism and the Limits of Justice*). But compare Kymlicka, "Community," in the same volume, 376f.

In the Charter's name it is also imposed over against the will of citizens and of local communities, as can be demonstrated from a good number of recent court decisions. It is imposed against age-old institutions such as marriage, which suddenly turn out to be discriminatory and hence unconstitutional.[63] It is even imposed in such a way that the distinction on which Trudeau rightly insisted – that between sin and crime – is erased. If something is not a crime it cannot be regarded, for public purposes, as a sin either. It is entitled to the state's support and to its own share of the people's pocketbook, whatever the people may think of it.[64]

The real justification for all of this is not a circumstance – that is, the new pluralist reality, which is not new at all – but a set of metaphysical judgments that lend themselves to a specific political philosophy. That philosophy aims at nothing less than a basic alteration in the foundations of social cohesion, which will no longer be laid out along its former axis: God, human dignity, family, personal and institutional freedom. The first and the third of these foundation stones must be removed, notwithstanding the fact that without them the second and the fourth cannot possibly hope to retain their shape or strength or alignment. The first and the third are offensive because they bind together means and ends, whereas liberal neutrality – unhappy with these ends, or with the vision of the good life that they nurture – insists that means and ends be separated, the former being regarded as public, the latter as merely private. To achieve this it is convenient to pretend that the problem with this axis is that the religions are always quarreling about it. That they quarrel about it because for the most part they think it the *right* axis is deliberately ignored. Ignored too, in this great ruse, is that in the pluralism of the liberal secularist another

---

63 See *Halpern et al. v. Attorney General of Canada et al.*, Court of Appeal for Ontario, 10 June 2003.

64 See further my commentary in the *National Post* ("To approve or not to approve," 27 December 2002) on *Chamberlain v. Surrey School District No. 36* [2002] 4 S.C.R. 710, and Chapter 6 (this volume).

and quite different conception of the good life (a broadly utilitarian, autonomy-oriented one) is already in play. The divorce of means from ends, or of the right from the good, belongs to that conception; but it is quite impossible on the theistic worldview of the major Western religions, just at it would have been impossible on the worldview of Plato or Aristotle.

We can hardly be surprised, then, when the state, in so far as it adopts the spurious, hegemonic "pluralism" of liberal secularism and seeks to enforce it, begins to appear not so much the neutral mediator as the enemy of religion; when it begins to look like the official guardian of agnosticism and atheism, or like the guarantor of freedom from religion rather than freedom of religion. When, in other words, it begins to privilege those belief systems whose primary article is the denial of the divine or of any practical or public knowledge of the divine. Nor should we be surprised if this course engenders, rather than prevents, a religious struggle that leads ultimately to scenes of civil disobedience.

This is only half the problem, however, and in mentioning it I have given only half my answer. The difficulty with even the most principled pluralism, for all its laudable commitment to preserving the particular – to honouring the actual religious and cultural forms of *religare* that constitute our different communities – is that it remains an abstraction. In fact, the more principled it is, and the harder it strives to re-narrate contractarianism's primal myth on a communitarian level, the more abstract it becomes. The state, however, has not the luxury of abstraction.[65] If, after refusing to accept the actual common ground between them, it is to succeed at holding together our different communities in a common society, it must itself produce a powerful form of *religare*. Rousseau

---

65 As Sandel, *Liberalism and the Limits of Justice*, 216f., observes, "democratic politics cannot long abide a public life as abstract and decorous, as detached from moral purposes, as Supreme Court opinions [etc.] are supposed to be. A politics that brackets morality and religion too thoroughly soon generates disenchantment."

understood this, in a way that modern secularists often do not, which is why he believed in civil religion.[66]

For her part, the modern secularist is left groping after Rousseau's god, who cannot be named. She too is committed to the *extra respublicam nulla salus*, even if translated into the language of globalism and of the NGOs. "Tolerance" means for her pretty much what it meant for Rousseau: only those who adhere to a particular set of social sentiments are worthy of participation in public life. And as these sentiments are reinforced with the symbols and sanctions of political power, the secularism she espouses takes on the shape and characteristics of civil religion. It not only competes with, but where necessary begins to repress, the inherited religious traditions of the nation and its citizenry. That is what it means to her to get beyond idols. Like Fenn, for whom the Sacred is really the self-deification of the secular, she is oblivious to the idol of her own making: the Idol to end all idolatry and, hence, all strife. "The false self-consciousness of the would-be secular society," says Oxford theologian Oliver O'Donovan, "lies in its determination to conceal the religious judgments that it has made."[67]

How far are we in Canada, to whom Fenn looks for relief from American civil religion, from our own version of life under *le Directoire?* A very long way, one may hope. Yet Wilson's

---

66 Kant too understood it, which is why he made such an effort to subjugate the positive religions to his own political vision; Hegel likewise. We may speak also, mutatis mutandis, of Comte, Troeltsch, Dewey, Durkheim, Bellah, Etzioni – all have seen the necessity for a political *religare* that is also a form of *religio*, not lacking for a cosmic or transcendent dimension. Some, of course, are searching for other ways to avoid a new round of theomachy (see, for example, Cairns et al., *Citizenship, Diversity and Pluralism*).

67 O'Donovan, *Desire of the Nations*, 247. Fenn, *Beyond Idols*, 8, argues that "to complete the process of secularization it will be necessary to remove any signs of the sacred that claim to be able to stand the test of time." But this would amount to nothing but the establishment of the civil religion he intends to reject.

remark lingers in the air, a query that has yet to receive a definitive response from the still-hazy future he sought to probe: "Whether indeed our own type of society will effectively maintain public order, without institutional coercion, once the persisting influence of past religion wanes even further, remains to be seen." Certainly in Canada there are disturbing signs of weakness in the churches and religious communities, to which analogies can be found in that dark moment of French history.[68] Moreover, there are equally disturbing signs of the state's willingness to interfere, chiefly through the stirrings of its judicial arm, in matters of religious freedom.

Ironically, today's instrument of choice for that interference is human rights, a fact that reveals the Janus-like nature of secularism. Secularism may be statist by inclination, or it may be libertarian; much of the time (as for Trudeau) it is both at once. In so far as it intends to resist the blandishments of statism it turns in d'Argenson's direction, emphasizing that "each man is perfectly free in all things that do no harm to others." Human rights arguments may then be deployed to limit the state's power over the individual, as the Charter intends. But in so far as these arguments are grounded in Enlightenment or Romantic notions of the autonomous individual, they require a corresponding *increase* in the power of the state, through its courts, to arbitrate the conflicting rights claims of its citizens and lobby groups.[69]

---

68 O'Donovan (224ff.) writes briefly but astutely on civil religion as a temptation to the church; Robert Kraynak at length, but less astutely, in *Christian Faith and Modern Democracy*. The 1934 Barmen Declaration, together with Karl Barth's famous *Theological Existence Today!* which was banned by the Nazi government that same year, still provide the paradigm of resistance.

69 Society, reconceived as "an acephalous organism" in the fashion of modern secularism, "dissolves its unity and coherence by replacing it with a plurality of 'rights,'" argues O'Donovan. Not that the language of subjective rights is unnecessary. "What is distinctive about the modern conception of rights, however, is that

And this power is sooner or later wielded against religious freedom, whether of individuals or of their communities. Which is to say, religious freedom – reduced to the uncertain status of "a Canadian value"[70] – is forced to bow to a state-enforced concept of human dignity, of the family, and of human community.[71]

In this light, it is surely not wrong to speak of secularism as a sublimation of civil religion, even of civil religion in its strong sense, the sense given it in *Du contrat social.* Secularism attributes competencies to the state that are, in their way, the equal of those claimed for it by Rousseau. Another telling piece of evidence can be found in the fact that contemporary secularists are inclined, like Rousseau, to identify orthodox Christianity (Roman Catholicism in particular) as their bête noir, the Beast that must be tamed. For orthodox Christianity,

---

subjective rights are taken to be original, not derived. The fundamental reality is a plurality of competing, unreconciled rights, and the task of law is to harmonise them" (*Desire of the Nations,* 246ff.). And he adds: "This picture is not significantly improved when, cross-breeding natural rights with legal positivism, it is said that the law must first *create* these promiscuous rights, then harmonise them." Which leads back to my point above; namely, that this situation ultimately requires a dramatic increase in the state's power if order is to be enforced against the chaos.

70 Thus former minister of justice Martin Cauchon, in his press release on the *Proposal for an Act respecting certain aspects of legal capacity for marriage* (17 July 2003). See also, for example, *Brillinger v. Brockie,* par. 46 (Ontario Superior Court, 17 June 2002, CFN 179/00), which appears to make freedom of religion a function of democratic freedom rather than the reverse.

71 In Charter terms, this is the triumph of section 15 over sections 1 and 2, enabled by a distorted concept of human dignity – that is, a strictly subjectivist concept of the kind one gets when the first of the foundation stones is removed – which has been imported into the Charter as an ideological framework for equality rights. See further my arguments in "Rights and Recognition," in Cere and Farrow, *Divorcing Marriage.*

in so far as it is orthodox, eschews the soul/body dualism, hence also the private/public dualism, which is the precondition for secularism as for civil religion. And it still dares to say *extra ecclesiam non sit salus.*

Does the solution to this problem – that is, to the curtailing of religious freedom by way of a state-imposed anthropology that threatens to bind us together by force of law – lie in an appeal to the preamble? I think it does, at least in part, though some may be skeptical about the success of such a strategy in the courts.[72] The preamble is part of Canada. It belongs to Canada, and Canada to it. And the preamble coordinates the rule of law itself to acknowledgment of the supremacy of God. Nevertheless, it must be acknowledged that the preamble, while it takes the right course and points us in the right direction, does so with a brevity Rousseau would have admired. Is the God of which it speaks the God of the Judeo-Christian tradition or something like Rousseau's deity, which serves only to support civic duty and to reinforce the power of the state? Does the preamble make love of the laws dependent on divine worship or does it put divine worship in the service of the laws?[73] Both semantically and historically the former view is clearly the legitimate one. Yet any appeal to the preamble will have to be wary of playing into

---

72 David Brown, at least, reaches the same conclusion ("Freedom From or Freedom For?" 615): "In order to ensure that freedom of religion remains a public right, courts should return and consider more carefully the challenge posed by the language of the *Charter's* Preamble. Far from being a 'dead letter,' the Preamble poses fundamental questions of political philosophy, including the relationship between the transcendental and the political order. Whether Canadian courts preserve the public nature of religious freedom may well depend on the extent to which they are prepared to engage in the debate mandated by the *Charter's* Preamble."

73 Is it, in other words, merely a prop for the "ceremonial deism" that, south of the border, even the US Supreme Court thinks harmless enough?

the hands of the civil religionists, be they in or out of the religion closet. Likewise it will have to be wary of conceding the dualisms just mentioned, or their counterpart in human rights theory, which is the conflation of freedom of religion with freedom of conscience.[74]

This brings me to my final point, which, since I have written about it elsewhere, may be expressed very briefly here. It concerns the use of the term "secular," which I do not think should be abandoned in the war against the idols but, rather, reclaimed. It also goes to the heart of the debate over the competency of the state in matters religious.

SECULARITY AS A REFUSAL OF CIVIL RELIGION

The former chief justice of Canada, Antonio Lamer, was wrong, I suggested earlier, to claim that Canadian society is essentially secular – wrong, that is, if we are using the word as he used it. But there is an older meaning of the word that would make Lamer right, at least from a Christian point of view.[75] That is because, from a Christian point of view, no society and no state is entitled any longer to be anything *but* secular. The descent and ascent of Jesus Christ, who suffers

---

74 The phrase "religious conscience," frequently employed in Chapter 2 (this volume), suggests such a conflation, which comes into play with Dickson's reading of "the purpose of freedom of conscience and religion" in *Big M.* Sandel, *Liberalism and the Limits of Justice*, xiii, understates the objection when he says: "Assimilating religious liberty to liberty in general reflects the liberal aspiration to neutrality ... [but] does not always serve religious liberty well." Besides confusing "the pursuit of preferences with the performance of duties," it effectively privatizes religion.

75 I do not hesitate to speak from a Christian point of view since, in the last analysis, I have no other. However, one does not need to share that point of view to find some merit, if merit there is, in what I am saying.

the ultimate political repression and accedes to the ultimate
political authority, who bears the final injustice and becomes
the final judge, spoils every state and every sovereignty of any
other ambition. It sets them under judgment; which is to say,
it secularizes them.

Here, of course, secularization does not indicate the process
"whereby religious thinking, practice, and institutions lose
social significance." Quite the contrary. The concomitant of
that sort of secularization turns out to be the deification of the
state. It is a counterfeit secularization, which Christianity can
and should expose as counterfeit. The secularization of which
Christianity speaks indicates rather the process by which political and juridical thinking, practice, and institutions are
denied the trajectory of self-deification.[76] That denial does not
mean that they lose their social significance for Christians,
much less that social significance itself becomes problematic
(à la Fenn); rather they gain in social significance, for a new
burden is placed upon them to act in the light of the knowledge of the divine justice and power revealed in Christ. But
that very knowledge limits their significance to that of a stew-
ard, whose authority is relative and temporary, not absolute.

This older notion of secularity, which takes seriously the
function of the state while carefully circumscribing its powers
and resisting its tendencies to self-aggrandizement, carries
with it no suggestion that the state should be indifferent to
religious concerns. As O'Donovan has observed, "secular" –
deriving from the Latin *saeculum*, meaning an age, era, or
generation – was not until relatively recent times interpreted
dualistically as the opposite of "sacred" or of "spiritual." Only
where the present age has itself been determined as somehow
cut off from the sacred or the spiritual could the word have
such a meaning. For classical Christianity the present age had
no such character; neither then did the word. Its counterpart
was not "sacred" but "eternal," meaning that which belongs to

---

76 Of course they may still choose to pursue it in practice, with such
   consequences as may follow.

the age to come, to the kingdom without end, towards which the present age looks in hope.[77]

My point is not merely a pedantic one, nor am I offering a lesson in Christian curiosities from a long-forgotten past. In making an appeal to the preamble I have been urging an end to secularism's false modesty about the state's rendering of religious judgments. It is not just that the state may and might render such judgments, but that in one way or another every state must and will. It therefore behooves it, and the society it serves, to be open about these judgments and about the grounds on which they rest.[78] The preamble affords a suitable

---

77 O'Donovan, *Desire of the Nations*, 211. Casanova, *Public Religions in the Modern World*, 13, grasps only imperfectly the point of this "historically rather unusual variant of the sacred-profane division"; which no doubt helps to explain his insistence (233f.) that Christianity capitulate, theologically, ethically, and politically, to the Enlightenment.

78 Let me revert once more to the marriage issue since it has become a lightning rod for controversy about church-state relations. Can anyone really suppose that this issue can be decided by the state without rendering a religious judgment of any kind? If the state offers same-sex "marriage," does it not reject the judgment of the major religions about the nature of marriage and adopt that of certain fringe religions? If the state instead abandons its own interest in marriage to the religions, does it not imply that it must depend upon them for the maintenance of a vital social institution – thus far endorsing and affirming them – or else deny their belief that it *is* vital? If, on the other hand, it opts for marriage as traditionally understood by the religions, does it not gratefully receive from them what they have thus provided it? Of course the state may say that it has its own non-religious reasons for its course of action, but how far can these non-religious reasons remain untainted by religious ones? The problem is particularly acute as soon as children come into view. Are *anyone's* views about children free of religious implications? And whose views will the state adopt? Mine? Peter Singer's? A Moloch devotee's? Whose will it enforce, and whose will it proscribe? No,

place to begin, or rather to resume, such an open conversation in Canada. But in making my appeal to the preamble I am equally concerned, indeed more concerned, to insist upon *a genuine modesty* in the state's exercise of religious judgment. This genuine modesty begins with honesty, with openness, but it requires something more than that. It requires an effective curb on the state's inherent tendency to subsume and sublate religion in the service of its own cause. This tendency works incognito through liberal secularism; it works more openly through civil religion, whether that of Rousseau or even that of Durkheim; and more openly yet in the repressive regimes of fascist and theocratic states. Christianity, though hardly immune and too often complicit, is one belief-system and one form of religion that, when functioning properly, offers such a curb.[79] It does not do so by denying the secular nature of Canadian society (or any other) but by insisting upon it, where "secular" means something like "limited in scope and force to this passing age," or "relativized by the truth and reality of the age to come."

On this eschatological view – which for convenience we may call modest secularism[80] – the secular state, with its responsibilities for public order during the present age, is required to face up to its provisionality, its limits, its temporary and partial

---

whatever the state does here, as also in embryology legislation, it cannot wash its hands of religion.

79 That it has not always functioned properly one must quickly concede: for example, when it encouraged the state to banish Jews simply for being Jews. I have offered a partial explanation of its past failures, from a theological point of view, in *Ascension and Ecclesia*; but obviously I do not accept the notion that Christianity is ordinarily given to civil religion. The wildly excessive accounts that one sometimes encounters (e.g., in Carroll's *Constantine's Sword*) do no service at all to the truth of the matter. One thing that has always to be examined, in a given situation, is what is happening to Christianity's eschatological proviso. Where this suffers – or is virtually obliterated, as in atheistic or theocratic states – enormous problems are sure to arise.

80 See n. 61 above.

stewardship of divine justice. So too is the church, in its stewardship of divine grace. On this view neither the church nor the state can rightly accord to itself absolute authority in the present age, because neither has the God-given mandate or means to do so. Because the doctrine of the Two is above all a doctrine of two ages, as O'Donovan says, it qualifies and limits both church and state, whose co-existence reminds each of its proper limits. In other words, the doctrine of the Two is not the source in human society of an unnecessary division or conflict but, rather, the source of a necessary restraint, of a healthy tension, between provisional and hence partial competencies and jurisdictions.[81]

This is the view of secularity that makes the best sense of the preamble. It is of course a Christian view, with deep roots in Canadian and European history. Yet it is a view capable of maintaining the right to freedom of religion for all citizens – a right that both civil religion and contemporary secularism undermine – while demolishing the latter's fiction that the state itself has no religious interests. It is a view capable of accommodating the fact that Christendom as a political consensus no longer exists and that a plurality of religions and worldviews vie for attention in shaping public policy, each trying to persuade adherents of the others that it has an important contribution to make to the common good. In recognizing this, however, it does not suppose that a society can function without some degree of consensus about that good, nor does it suppose that just any consensus will do. Indeed it does not think it a matter of indifference whether a society officially acknowledges this God or that or (contrary to the constitution) no God at all. It is always ready to argue for its own view of the good and to speak of the God in which it believes as well as to listen to the views of others. And it recognizes, or at least strives to recognize, what is at stake in our collective decisions about such things.

---

81 The tension is by nature a precarious one; but it is a false, if highly successful, myth that this tension is itself the source of disease in Western civilization, the root of all conflict.

To clarify further this approach to secular polity, especially as it pertains to the interpretation and application of a document like the Charter of Rights and Freedoms, one would need to set out a theory of freedom and a theory of rights that did not concede that the right to freedom of religion is grounded either in the individual or in democratic principles. Were I to try that myself, I would want to begin, I think, with Tertullian's attempt to derive *libertatem religionis* from the nature of religion rather than from the self-possession of the person,[82] and proceed by replacing d'Argenson's restrictive maxim with another and more generous one. In place of "each man is perfectly free in all things that do no harm to others," I would put Augustine's principle of cooperative order, "that we harm no one and do good to whomever we can."[83] This principle is closely allied to another; namely, the principle of modesty that Augustine derives from the incarnation: "power, for its part, should follow justice and not precede it."[84] But that is for another volume and another time. From the present one, I trust, sufficient good may already be derived.

---

82 The latter being given in and with the former; compare *Apologeticus* 24 and 28. John Owen (*Works* VIII, 184; noted in Gunton, *Promise of Trinitarian Theology*, 84) cites Tertullian as follows: *Nec religionis est cogere religionem, quae sponte suscipi debent, non vi.* This is one of the earliest explicit arguments for religious freedom.

83 *City of God* 19.14. This political maxim, like the following juridical one, ought not to offend even the most ardent secularist. Yet it owes its appearance to theological argumentation.

84 *Trin.* 13.17: *Potentia quippe adiuncta iustitiae, vel iustitia accedente potentiae, iudiciariam potestatem facit. Pertinet autem iustitia ad voluntatem bonam: unde dictum est ab Angelis nato Christo:* Gloria in excelsis Deo, et in terra pax hominibus bonae voluntatis. *Potentia vero sequi debet iustitiam, non praeire: ideo et in rebus secundis ponitur, id est prosperis: "secundae" autem a "sequendo" sunt dictae.* Edmund Hill (in Saint Augustine, *The Trinity* [Brooklyn: New City Press, 1991], 367f., n. 36) refers us back here to Augustine's treatment of the fall "as the archetype of all social disarray, in which what is private is disastrously preferred to what is common to the whole human community."

Postscript

In *Public Religions in the Modern World*, José Casanova questions
the secularization thesis of Wilson and, indeed, of Mills and
Marx and Durkheim and Weber. Who, he asks, still believes
the founding myth of sociology, the myth of secularization?[1]
There has been a long and complex process of differentiation
between the religious and the secular spheres – between the
church, on the one hand, and the state, the economy, and the
sciences on the other, not to speak of education and the arts
– which has led to the autonomy of the latter and the disestablishment of the former in what used to be called Christendom.
But religion has not died out; it is alive and well. What is more,
it is alive and well in the public sphere, often closely engaged
with civil society. If there was a period of the so-called privatization of religion, it has now given way to deprivatization. Secularized society and its religious communities co-exist and
interact in all sorts of fruitful ways.

Casanova is not alone. As intimated earlier, there are many
sociologists today – presumably those confident that the discipline itself, like the religions of which it was once dismissive,
can survive demythologizing quite nicely – who think that the
struggle between the secular and the religious is rapidly
becoming a thing of the past, with no need to declare a winner

---

1 p. 11.

and a loser.[2] That judgment may be hasty, if recent indications are anything to go by; it may also be somewhat disingenuous.[3] But absent a clear and common understanding of its terms it must in any case be doubtful; and it is plain enough from the present volume that "secular," like "religious," is a term for which a clear and common definition is difficult to give. That is one of the challenges with which *Recognizing Religion in a Secular Society* leaves us, though fortunately we are also left with considerable resources for facing it.

There is another problem with Casanova's optimistic picture, however, that compounds the difficulty. If "secular" is not to have a religion-exclusive sense, as Iain Benson puts it, then the autonomy to which it points must be a relative one. But relative how? Each of the contributors to this volume has wrestled with that question in his or her own way. The results, like the starting points, have varied.

Working with a "dialectic of normative commitments" that posits law and religion as two fully autonomous spheres, Beverley McLachlin has attempted to relativize each to the other not by appealing to the religious basis of law but by appealing to the legal basis for the manifestation of religion. At least two questions arise here, one concerning the foundations of law, the other concerning the nature of religion as thus provided for by law. The former may be put in terms of the Charter preamble and answered in explication or rejection thereof, as the final chapter suggests. The latter may be put in terms of the distinction between freedom of conscience and freedom of religion, a distinction arguably endangered by the Lockean tradition; or with Jean Elshtain, it may be put in terms of the relation between religion as a concern of the individual and religion as a corporate or body politic. However

---

2 "This study maintains that the age of secular-religious cleavages, of struggles over the historical process of modern secularization, has basically come to an end in the historical area of Western Christendom" (ibid. 220).

3 In Casanova's sophisticated and fascinating work, I do not think it disingenuous; but compare Chapter 9, n. 77 (this volume).

these questions are put (and in retrospect we can see that they are pressed upon us from a number of different angles) it is evident that the weight of opinion among the other contributors is against according to the law, or to the state generally, a comprehensive autonomy of this kind.

Tristram Engelhardt's approach, allowing for differences in subject matter, looks almost like the opposite of McLachlin's. Engelhardt points out that the state that acknowledges no religious basis – that lays too much stress on its autonomy – is forced to derive its authority entirely, if not from raw force, then from the consent of its citizens. This is not meant as a compliment but as a cause for concern. For consent requires consensus, and in the absence of recognized transcendent criteria for moral judgments, only a very limited sort of consensus is possible. Under such circumstances we can only search for equally limited political and juridical structures, devoted chiefly to facilitating (not imposing) cooperation between discrete moral communities. Religion, in other words, making the transcendent claims that foster functioning moral communities, will carve out a space for those forms of broader social cooperation that are deemed possible in a situation of irresolvable moral conflict; that is, in the face of the discordant pluralism thrust upon us by the inherently divisive nature of irreligion. Of this more pessimistic account of the secular, and far more limited view of the state, questions may also be asked, of course. Will the highest common denominator between opposing communities prove high enough for a relatively peaceful co-existence? What exactly may be done to encourage that? What political criteria should govern the structures of cooperation that a limited constitutional democracy can still hope to develop? And what are the implications of these criteria for the evolution of jurisprudence? How far is our jurisprudence adaptable to this modus vivendi approach, or to a situation of irresolvable moral difference?[4]

---

4 These are questions that might be put to Iain Benson, who also turns in this direction via his appeal to John Gray's *modus vivendi*

Neither William Galston nor David Novak adopt anything quite so radical as Engelhardt's pluralism. Yet Galston's "politics of recognition" and Novak's communitarian version of the social contract also seek to curtail the state's autonomous tendencies, questioning its right to stand over and above primal human communities or even civil associations. Like Engelhardt, both posit an irreducible pluralism in which these communities neither derive their authority from the state nor cede the greater part of it to the state; rather, they share *with* the state only what is appropriate for the latter as a secondary or servant polity. Something similar may be said respecting civil society. In Galston's words, "the common good of a pluralist society is not merely the aggregate of individual and group interests, but it is not and must not be a *comprehensive* good either." It therefore does not trump the good of its primal communities, whose divided loyalties are a healthy ingredient in the recipe for an appropriately modest state.[5]

There are differences between Galston and Novak, however. For the former, the secular political order "is not simply a framework within which individuals, families, and associations may pursue their own purposes," whereas for the latter that would seem to be the case.[6] And while both men presuppose a working distinction "between basic human goods, which the state must defend, and diverse conceptions of flourishing above that base-line, which the state should accommodate to the maximum extent possible" (Galston), Novak more clearly posits a religious foundation for these basic goods, at least where social order is concerned. Moreover, he insists that both the rational

---

liberalism over against a more hegemonic "convergence liberalism" – hegemonic particularly where it waves most vigorously the banner of secularism.

5 In language similar to that of the final chapter, Novak adds the note of provisionality: "Democracy's goals cease to be democratic when they are made into anything more than penultimate temporal ends."

6 See 55ff.

grounds and the moral fibre for resisting the self-aggrandizement of the state are to be found precisely in religion. "The only cultural minorities who can resist the inner tendency of the secular state to turn all alternative societies into private corporations within its own purview ... are religious minorities."[7]

This raises the autonomy/relativity question in a new way. There can be no doubt that all societies depend on moral traditions that owe much to religion. But how far is that to be acknowledged? And is the debt merely a past one or does the borrowing continue? According to Margaret Somerville, it must indeed continue, particularly as modern technology thrusts up ever more pressing moral challenges for us to face. Yet it appears that this borrowed capital must somehow be laundered in order to protect the state's rightful autonomy, which is threatened if religion is used directly in the formation of public policy, even on matters of life and death. For Somerville civil society is the "multivoiced" forum through which the insights of religion into human nature are secularized and, thus, safely mediated to the state's policy makers. For some of the other contributors, however, the line is not so readily drawn, whether between civil society and the state or between religious and secular thought. Religiously grounded conceptions of human life may and sometimes must pass over into public policy deliberations, even at the level of the state and of international politics, if those deliberations are to be meaningful.

We may think here not only of Prince Hassan's carefully balanced contribution at the beginning, or of the more provocative claims of the final chapter, but of Jean Elshtain's contribution in the middle. Elshtain offers us, by way of

---

7 Novak's explanation bears repetition: "Membership in these traditional communities is outside the range of civil society because of their historical precedence, and it is above the range of civil society because of the ontological status given these communities through their relationship with God. Indeed, these communities claim both ancient and cosmic privileges. This is what both limits the secular and, within its limited range, entitles it."

illustration, the basic notion of human dignity – chief among the hypergoods identified by Beverley McLachlin – in which all talk of human rights must be lodged. This notion cannot be a free-floating one, she says, if it is to anchor and maintain the principles of human rights. But where will it come to rest if not in assertions (respecting the *imago dei*, for example) that can hardly avoid the label "religious"? Or take the concept of freedom of religion itself. Elshtain does not merely argue that freedom of religion is the first among freedoms. She also asks us to consider the view that freedom of religion is self-grounding: not the gift *to* religion from a pluralist and democratic polity but the gift *of* religion in support of such a polity (indeed, of any polity willing to reckon with it). And if human dignity, with its attendant rights and freedoms, is ultimately a religious concept, then at the very point where modern democratic states like to pride themselves on their moral relevance, not to say their moral superiority, their autonomy is seen to be anything but absolute.

This invites a concluding remark, if a concluding remark is possible in so rich a volume. *Recognizing Religion in a Secular Society* situates itself not so much between Wilson and Casanova as outside their frame of reference and as a challenge to it. Though very different in aspect, the latter remain within the orbit of those familiar words from Locke's *Letter on Toleration*: "I esteem it above all things necessary to distinguish exactly the business of civil government from that of religion and to settle the just bounds that lie between the one and the other." But how shall we distinguish exactly, if the interests of religion interpenetrate with those of civil society, and those of civil society with those of the state? The present book, unembarrassed by the risks of its interdisciplinarity, explores this more perichoretic reality with the vigour characteristic of each of its contributors. It may not answer, but it does not shy away from, the question of relativity – that is, of both autonomy and heteronomy. For only when that question is faced is it possible to comprehend either the public nature of the religions or the nature of what we too glibly call secular society.

Contributors

IAIN T. BENSON
Executive Director, Centre for Cultural Renewal

JEAN BETHKE ELSHTAIN
The Laura Spelman Rockefeller Professor of Social and
Political Ethics, University of Chicago

H. TRISTRAM ENGELHARDT, JR
Professor of Philosophy, Rice University and Professor
Emeritus, Baylor College of Medicine

DOUGLAS FARROW
Associate Professor of Christian Thought, McGill University

WILLIAM GALSTON
Professor, School of Public Affairs, University of Maryland
and Director, Institute for Philosophy and Public Policy

THE RIGHT HONOURABLE BEVERLEY
MCLACHLIN, P.C.
Chief Justice of Canada

DAVID NOVAK
J. Richard and Dorothy Shiff Chair of Jewish Studies, and
Professor of Philosophy, University of Toronto

MARGARET SOMERVILLE
Samuel Gale Professor of Law and Founding Director,
Centre for Medicine, Ethics, and Law, McGill University

H.R.H. PRINCE EL HASSAN BIN TALAL
Chairman of the Royal Institute for Inter-Faith Studies
The Hashemite Kingdom of Jordan

Bibliography

Aston, Nigel. *Religion and Revolution in France, 1780–1804*. Washington: Catholic University of America Press, 2000.

Barfield, Owen. *Speaker's Meaning*. Middletown: Wesleyan University Press, 1967

Barth, Karl. *Theological Existence Today! A Plea for Theological Freedom*. Trans. R. Birch Hoyle. London, Hodder and Stoughton, 1933.

Baum, Gregory. *Religion and Alienation: A Theological Reading of Sociology*. New York: Paulist Press, 1975.

Bayertz, Kurt, ed. *The Concept of Moral Consensus*. Dordrecht: Kluwer, 1994.

Beauchamp, Tom L., and James F. Childress. *Principles of Biomedical Bioethics*. New York: Oxford University Press, 1979

Brooks, Rodney. *Flesh and Machines: How Robots Will Change Us*. New York: Pantheon Books, 2002.

Cairns, Alan, John C. Courtney, Peter MacKinnon, Hans J. Michelmann, and David E. Smith, eds. *Citizenship, Diversity and Pluralism: Canadian and Comparative Perspectives*. Montreal: McGill-Queen's University Press, 2000.

Carroll, James. *Constantine's Sword: The Church and the Jews – A History*. Boston: Houghton Mifflin, 2001.

Casanova, José. *Public Religions in the Modern World*. Chicago: University of Chicago Press, 1994.

Cere, Daniel, and Douglas Farrow, eds. *Divorcing Marriage: Unveiling the Dangers in Canada's New Social Experiment*. Kitchener: Castle Quay/Augsburg Fortress, 2004.

Cristi, Marcela. *From Civil to Political Religion: The Intersection of Culture, Religion and Politics.* Waterloo: Wilfrid Laurier University Press, 2001.

Daniels, Norman, ed. *Reading Rawls: Critical Studies on Rawls'* A Theory of Justice. Oxford: Blackwell, 1975 .

Dworkin, Ronald. *Taking Rights Seriously.* Cambridge, MA: Harvard University Press, 1978.

Eisenach, Eldon. *The Next Religious Establishment: National Identity and Political Theology in Post-Protestant America.* Lanham, MD: Rowman and Littlefield, 2000.

Eliade, Mircea. *The Sacred and the Profane: The Nature of Religion.* New York: Harcourt Brace and Co., 1957.

Engelhardt, H. Tristram Jr. *The Foundations of Bioethics.* 2nd ed. New York: Oxford University Press, 1996.

– *The Foundations of Christian Bioethics.* Lisse, Holland: Swets and Zeitlinger, 2000.

Engelhardt, H. Tristram, Jr, and A. L. Caplan, eds. *Scientific Controversies: Case Studies in the Resolution and Closure of Disputes in Science and Technology.* New York: Cambridge University Press, 1987.

Fackenheim, Emil L. *The Religious Dimension in Hegel's Thought.* Bloomington: University of Indiana Press, 1967.

Farrow, Douglas. *Ascension and Ecclesia: On the Significance of the Doctrine of the Ascension for Ecclesiology and Christian Cosmology.* Edinburgh: T. and T. Clark, 1999.

Fenn, Richard K. *Beyond Idols: The Shape of a Secular Society.* New York: Oxford University Press, 2001.

Filibeck, Giorgio, ed. *Human Rights in the Teaching of the Church: From John XXIII to John Paul II.* Vatican City: Libreria Editrice Vaticana, 1994.

Foley, Kathleen, and Herbert Hendin, eds. *The Case against Assisted Suicide. For the Right to End-of-Life Care.* Baltimore: Johns Hopkins University Press, 2002.

Fukuyama, Francis. *The Great Disruption: Human Nature and the Reconstitution of Social Order.* London: Free Press, 1999.

Furedi, Frank. *The New Ideology of Imperialism: Renewing the Moral Imperative.* London: Pluto Press, 1994.

Galston, William. *Liberal Pluralism: The Implications of Value Pluralism for Political Theory and Practice.* New York: Cambridge University Press, 2002.

Geertz, Clifford. *The Interpretation of Cultures: Selected Essays.* New York: HarperCollins, 1973.

Glendon, Mary Ann. *Rights Talk: The Impoverishment of Political Discourse.* New York: Free Press, 1992.

Good, Graham. *Humanism Betrayed: Theory, Ideology and Culture in the Contemporary University.* Montreal: McGill-Queens University Press, 2001.

Goodin, Robert E., and Philip Pettit, eds. *A Companion to Contemporary Political Philosophy.* Oxford: Blackwell, 1995.

Grabbe, Lester L. *Judaism from Cyrus to Hadrian.* Vol. 1. Minneapolis: Fortress Press, 1992.

Gray, John. *Two Faces of Liberalism.* New York: The New Press, 2000.

Gunton, Colin. *The Promise of Trinitarian Theology.* Edinburgh, T. and T. Clark, 1991.

Habermas, Jürgen *The Future of Human Nature.* Trans. H. Beister and W. Rehg. Malden: Polity Press, 2003.

Hashmi, S.H., ed. *Islamic Political Ethics: Civil Society, Pluralism, and Conflict.* Princeton: Princeton University Press, 2002.

Herbert, David. *Religion and Civil Society: Rethinking Public Religion in the Contemporary World.* Aldershot: Ashgate, 2003.

Hirst, Paul Q., ed. *The Pluralist Theory of the State: Selected Writings of G.D.H. Cole, J.N. Figgis, and H.J. Laski.* London: Routledge, 1989.

Hogg, Peter W. *Canada Act 1982 Annotated.* Toronto: Carswell, 1986.

Holyoake, George Jacob. *English Secularism: A Confession of Belief.* Chicago: Open Court Publishing Co., 1896.

Horowitz, Asher, and Gad Horowitz. *"Everywhere They Are in Chains": Political Theory from Rousseau to Marx.* Scarborough: Nelson, 1988.

Hunter, James Davison. *Culture Wars: The Struggle to Define America.* New York: Basic Books, 1991.

Huntington, Samuel P. *The Clash of Civilizations and the Remaking of World Order.* New York: Touchstone, 1997.

Jonsen, Albert. *The Birth of Bioethics.* New York: Oxford University Press, 1998.

Kahn, Paul W. *The Cultural Study of Law: Reconstructing Legal Scholarship.* Chicago: University of Chicago Press, 1999.

Keown, John. *Euthanasia, Ethics and Public Policy: An Argument against Legalisation.* Cambridge: Cambridge University Press, 2002.

Kraynak, Robert P. *Christian Faith and Modern Democracy: God and Politics in the Fallen World.* Notre Dame: University of Notre Dame Press, 2001.

Küng, Hans, and Karl-Josef Kuschel, eds. *A Global Ethic: The Declaration of the Parliament of the World's Religions.* London: SCM Press, 1993.

Kymlicka, Will. *Contemporary Political Philosophy: An Introduction.* 2nd ed. New York: Oxford University Press, 2002.

Lee, Soon Ok. *Eyes of the Tailless Animals: Prison Memoirs of a North Korean Woman.* Bartlesville, OK: Living Sacrifice Book Company, 1999.

Livingston, James C. *Modern Christian Thought.* Vol. 1: *The Enlightenment and the Nineteenth Century.* 2nd ed. Upper Saddle River: Prentice-Hall, 1997.

Lyons, David, and Marguerite Van Die, eds. *Rethinking Church, State, and Modernity: Canada between Europe and America.* Toronto: University of Toronto Press, 2000.

Macedo, Stephen. *Diversity and Distrust: Civic Education in a Multicultural Democracy.* Cambridge, MA: Harvard University Press, 2000.

MacIntyre, Alasdair. *After Virtue: A Study in Moral Theory.* 2nd ed. Notre Dame: University of Notre Dame Press, 1984.

– *Whose Justice? Which Rationality?* Notre Dame: University of Notre Dame Press, 1988.

McConnell, Michael W., John H. Garvey, and Thomas C. Berg,. *Religion and the Constitution.* New York: Aspen Publishers, 2002.

McConkey, Dale, and Peter Augustine Lawler, eds. *Faith, Morality, and Civil Society.* Lanham: Lexington Books, 2003.

McLaren, J., and H. Coward, eds. *Religious Conscience, the State, and the Law: Historical Contexts and Contemporary Significance.* Albany: SUNY, 1999.

Maritain, Jacques. *The Rights of Man and Natural Law.* Trans. D. C. Anson. San Francisco: Ignatius Press, 1986.

Milbank, John, Catherine Pickstock, and Graham Ward, eds. *Radical Orthodoxy: A New Theology.* London: Routledge, 1999.

Misztal, B.A. *Trust in Modern Societies: The Search for the Bases of Social Order.* Cambridge, MA: Polity Press, 1998.

Nicholls, David. *The Pluralist State.* London: Macmillan, 1975.

Novak, David. *Natural Law in Judaism: The Idea of the Chosen People.* Cambridge: Cambridge University Press, 1998.

– *The Election of Israel.* Cambridge: Cambridge University Press, 1995.

O'Donovan, Oliver. *Resurrection and Moral Order: An Outline for Evangelical Ethics.* Grand Rapids: Eerdmans, 1986.

– *The Desire of the Nations: Rediscovering the Roots of Political Theology.* New York: Cambridge University Press, 1996.

O'Donovan, Oliver, and Joan O'Donovan. *From Irenaeus to Grotius: A Sourcebook in Christian Political Thought.* Grand Rapids: Eerdmans, 1999.

Olyan, S.M., and M.C. Nussbaum, eds. *Sexual Orientation and Human Rights in American Religious Discourse.* New York: Oxford University Press, 1998.

Pelletier, Louise, and Alberto Pérez-Gomez, eds. *Architecture, Ethics and Technology.* Montreal: McGill-Queen's University Press, 1994.

Percy, Walker. *Lost in the Cosmos.* New York: Farrer, Straus and Giroux, 1983.

Perry, Michael. *The Idea of Human Rights.* New York: Oxford University Press, 1998.

Potter, Van Rensselaer. *Bioethics: Bridge to the Future.* Englewood Cliffs, NJ: Prentice-Hall, 1971.

– *Global Bioethics.* East Lansing: Michigan State University Press, 1988.

Rawls, John. *Political Liberalism.* New York: Columbia University Press, 1996

– *A Theory of Justice.* Rev. ed. Cambridge, MA: Harvard University Press, 1999.

Robertson, D.B., ed. *Voluntary Associations: A Study of Groups in Free Societies.* Richmond: John Knox Press, 1966.

Rorty, Richard. *Contingency, Irony, and Solidarity.* New York: Cambridge University Press, 1989.

– *Truth and Progress: Philosophical Papers.* Vol. 3. Cambridge: Cambridge University Press, 1998.

Rousseau, Jean-Jacques. *On the Social Contract. With Geneva Manuscript and Political Economy.* Ed. R. D. Masters. Trans. J. R. Masters. New York: St Martin's, 1978.

Sandel, Michael J. *Democracy's Discontent:* America in Search of a Public Philosophy. Cambridge, MA: Harvard University Press, 1996.

– *Liberalism and the Limits of Justice.* 2nd ed. Cambridge: Cambridge University Press, 1998.

Shortt, A., and A. Doughty. *Documents Relating to the Constitutional History of Canada, 1759–1791.* Ottawa: King's Printer, 1907.

Skillen, James W., and Rockne M. McCarthy, eds. *Political Order and the Plural Structure of Society.* Atlanta: Scholars Press, 1991.

Smith, Christian, ed. *The Secular Revolution: Power, Interests and Conflict in the Secularization of American Public Life.* Berkeley: University of California Press, 2003.

Smith, Nicholas H. *Charles Taylor: Meaning, Morals and Modernity.* Oxford: Blackwell, 2002.

Somerville, Margaret. *The Ethical Canary: Science, Society and the Human Spirit.* Toronto: Viking Press, 2000.

– *Death Talk: The Case against Euthanasia and Physician-Assisted Suicide.* Montreal: McGill-Queen's University Press, 2001.

Sakharov, Sophrony. *We Shall See Him as He is.* Rev. ed. Trans. Rosemary Edmonds. Maldon, UK: Monastery of St. John the Baptist, 1988.

Soroush, Abdolkarim. *Reason, Freedom and Democracy in Islam: Essential Writings of Abdolkarim Soroush.* Trans. Mahmoud Sadri. Oxford: Oxford University Press, 2000.

bin Talal, Hassan, and Alain Elkann, *Essere Musulmano.* Bompiani: Milan, 2001.

Taylor, Charles. *Sources of the Self: The Making of the Modern Identity.* Cambridge, MA: Harvard University Press, 1989.

– *Multiculturalism.* Princeton, Princeton University Press, 1994.

Teilhard de Chardin, Pierre. *The Future of Man.* London: Collins, 1964.

Tönnies, Ferdinand. *Community and Society.* Trans. C.P. Loomis. East Lansing: Michigan State University Press, 1957.

Vattimo, Gianni. *The End of Modernity.* Trans. Jon R. Snyder. Baltimore: Johns Hopkins University Press, 1988.

Vlachos, Hierotheos S. *The Mind of the Orthodox Church.* Trans. Esther Williams. Levadia: Birth of the Theotokos Monastery, 1998.

Wilson, Bryan R. *Religion in Secular Society: A Sociological Comment.* London: C.A. Watts and Co., 1966.

Witte, John Jr. *Religion and the American Constitutional Experiment: Essential Rights and Liberties.* Boulder: Westview Press, 2000.

Wright, N. Thomas. *The Resurrection of the Son of God.* Vol. 3: *Christian Origins and the Question of God.* Minneapolis: Fortress Press, 2003.

Index